| new magic fo

how to live a c

TOM EVANS

| NEW MAGIC FOR A NEW ERA |

1st edition, published 2015
ISBN 978-1-849146470

Front cover images ©albisoima and ©sahuad via www.fotolia.com.
Tarot images used with the kind permission of the Builders of the Adytum.
Crystal energy symbols used with the kind permission of the Kryon School in
Germany.
Book Layout ©2013 BookDesignTemplates.com

Published by Tmesis Ltd | www.tmesis.co

*to Louise, my rock, best buddy,
soul mate and humangel*

| silos |

| preamble |

THIS IS A DIFFERENT KIND OF BOOK OF MAGIC.

This book won't teach you about sleight-of-hand magic.

It won't even tell you how to work out what someone is thinking with the magic of sleight-of-mind.

The magic explored here is more subtle and ethereal than that. It's the magic that leads us to living a charmed life. As intangible as that may sound, this type of magic leads to real world, tangible results.

It's the kind of magic that is as old as the hills, if not a little older.

It's not a given that life has to be tough. There is no conspiracy of a world out to get you, unless you want there to be one. The Universe is a kind and benevolent place. If it wasn't, we would not even be here.

This book is not so much a How To Do book but a How To Be book. When we get out of our own way, magic opens doors for us that take us down new and unimaginable paths.

Just try and imagine a world wilder than your wildest dreams. We can't. A magical world exists for all of us, which is grander and more exquisite than we can possibly imagine.

Rather than exploring this kind of magic theoretically, this book is immensely practical. Just imagine conjuring up the right amount of money into your world. Imagine having as much time as you need. Imagine loving what you do and being with the ones you love.

Find out how dis-ease is merely a symptom that leads to disease. Discover how we can heal the past, the present, and the future at the same time. Learn why we should appreciate adversity for the learnings it brings.

So dream on and dream up. Let me share with you some amazing tales, which took a bored techie guy down a road he did not know even existed. It's a road, too, which is opening up to even greater vistas.

This new kind of magic leads to a new era where we can bring even more of heaven down to earth.

NOTES FOR READERS

Each of the themes explored here is a separate silo. As such, you can dip in anywhere and take in a chapter that grabs your fancy. You can even read the book backwards. Naturally, you can just read it forwards too.

Each chapter follows a simple structure:

- Some explorations of an aspect of magic
- How I use it in my life
- The catch as to why sometimes the magic doesn't work
- How you can use it in yours

Horizontally in this book, you will notice there are spaces between each word. Vertically, you will notice that there are spaces between lines and paragraphs. You will, of course, see these in all books. Only in very few books, this being one of them, do these spaces contain content.

This book is magical and, as such, oozing from the space between the words is the magic to allow the wisdom that comes from the words and sentences to enter into your life. You would be right at this point to ask how and why I can make such a claim.

Well, here's the thing about magic, whether it is sleight-of-hand, sleight-of-mind, or real magick. All magic tricks are only magic tricks until you know how they are done. I learned this one from a book that did the same.

In many magic circles, it is customary that the magic is retained by a select few acolytes and controlled by adepts.

The reasons for this are twofold:

1. To stop the magic from falling into the wrong hands and being subsequently abused
2. For the keepers of such power to use it to wield illusory power over others

This magic book is different in two regards:

1. The magic is intrinsically safe to be used and shared freely
2. In this new era it is the right time for this magic to return to the Earth Plane

There is a tradition in occult circles that the 'student' must learn and discover some of the bigger keys for themselves. For this reason, occult teachings are full of blinds and mistakes. When you spot them, you not only understand why they are there, but really comprehend the teachings.

I have not purposely put blinds into this book, and hope there aren't any errors, but it's fair to say there is much more I haven't said about magic than I have said. Partly, this is because I want the book to be introductory, and partly for reasons of safety for the reader.

To help you on your way, this book contains some breadcrumbs for readers interested in learning even more.

BREADCRUMB : *they look like this*

At the end of each chapter you will find a symbol. Stare at it for about a minute and you will find it will lead you to more revelations all in good time.

Above all have fun.

IN LVX

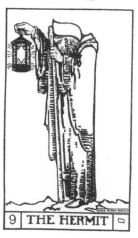

| no hell and back |

THERE ARE MANY FABULOUS PERSONAL DEVELOPMENT BOOKS THAT TELL OF A PERSON'S ENLIGHTENMENT THROUGH SOME TUMULTUOUS JOURNEY. INDEED, I HAVE LOST COUNT OF THE AUTHORS WHO I HAVE PERSONALLY MENTORED TO HELP TELL SUCH TALES.

Some people have been subject to horrible abuse and have grown in stature as a result of it. They might have been bullied or in an abusive relationship. The abuse may have been self-inflicted. Those that extricate themselves from these shadow worlds often show amazing compassion and forgiveness. Many end up helping others suffering from a similar plight.

Others have been on gruelling and exciting journeys, performing feats of extreme endurance and even survival. I've walked 26 miles around London in a bra, just the once, but those that have undertaken multiple marathons have my utmost admiration. If you have rowed across the oceans or scaled the highest peaks, my hat is off to you.

To those intrepid explorers, thanks for sharing your stories and what you learned from doing it so that I don't have to.

Some people recover from life-threatening illnesses, or horrendous accidents, and live to tell their tales. People who have fought in wars, have stared death right in the face, and may have even ended the lives of others. If you have been to the brink and stared over the precipice, so glad to have you back and thanks for sharing what you learned.

I have even met some people who have 'seen the light' in a Near-Death Experience. They often meet off-world intelligences and some even come back to the Earth Plane with one or more attached. Not only do they survive the un-survivable, but they come back with new skills and super-sensibilities. This is magic in action.

For some, life is just tough. They struggle from day to day to make ends meet. Some are in dead end jobs, and some in no jobs at all. Some wonder what the point of everything is. Some harbour doubts and fears, and have a lack of self-worth.

Amazingly, an increasing number of people live alone. Some out of choice, others simply because the love of their life hasn't shown up. They may have kissed lots of frogs but haven't yet met their prince or princess.

To numb the pain, we take pills, take to the bottle, smoke, eat, watch TV, and play computer games. We do all we can to escape from what we call reality.

Some of those who got entrapped in, and addicted to, these alternate realities have escaped back to help others so ensnared.

Now, I am well aware I am writing this all from the perspective of someone living in the so-called First World. Many people live at a whole other level of basic survival, not knowing where the next meal or drink of water is coming from. Even if you cannot even read and never get to read this particular book, I would like these people to know that I am writing this book for you too. My hope is that by spreading the magic to those who can 'get it', we can collectively create even more heaven on earth so that poverty, hunger, wars, and strife can be eliminated at a global level.

We are at an amazing point in our evolution. We have amazing mastery over the Physical Plane. Humankind are truly alchemists. We have even left the planet and looked back at the blue-green jewel of Spaceship Earth. We now know that we live on a small rock revolving around an averagely sized star. Our star is one of billions in our galaxy, and our galaxy one of a billion galaxies. At the time of writing, as far as we know, we are the sole self-aware beings in the whole of creation. No wonder some people feel a bit lonely.

We have even come to a point where we can dictate and design the next stages of our own evolution. Some scientists are actively engaged in tinkering with our DNA to do just this. Others are working out how to bolt technology on to our physiology and neurology to enhance our abilities, and to overcome some dis-abilities.

This is a book about how to undertake a personal transformation of a different, more subtle yet more powerful, nature. It is a book of alchemy that shows how we can transform and transmute who and what we are so that we can live our lives differently.

I've written ten books already, exploring some of these potentialities. None of these books, though, tell my story explicitly, although the content and themes of said books themselves are indicative of my own journey.

I have to say that my life so far has been most pleasant. For sure, I've had a few ups and downs and some sad times. I've loved and lost, and lost some loved ones along the way. I've thrown my toys out of the pram working for and with not-so-nice people. I'm critical of myself, harbour self-doubt, and am fearful of making an idiot of myself. At the same time, I don't like being criticised, and only cherish Four and Five star reviews on Amazon for my books. Three stars and less just won't do!

In general though, I've been blessed with a pretty good life. I would even go so far as to say that it's been a very fortuitous existence.

I've been in a loving relationship for over thirty years. I live in a lovely house in a beautiful part of the world, without any debt. I haven't retired, but I don't do what I call work as I only do what I love doing. If I need any cash, some money arrives. Likewise, all the resources I ever need seem to turn up out of the blue, just when I need them.

I am not an ascetic. I enjoy a pint of beer and a glass or three of wine. I love both cooking and eating gastronomic delights.

I'm not plagued by any allergies or food intolerances. I don't particularly like shellfish and I have learned whisky doesn't like me. I don't have a story to tell about how life was terrible and how I overcame a terrible hardship. For me, life hasn't been that hard, although I like to think I 'work' hard and am diligent in what I do.

This brings me to this book's Whats and Whys.

This book throws down the gauntlet by asking a few Whats.

- What would life be like if it wasn't so tough?
- What might we achieve individually, and collectively, if our wildest dreams came to pass?
- What sort of world could we live in?
- What would you do if you had more than enough time?
- What might you do if money was no object?

This book aims to help you turn over a new leaf (geddit?), by asking some Whys.

- Why do we make life so difficult for ourselves?
- Why do other people seem to be luckier in love and life?
- Why does life throw us a curved ball, just when we least expect it and need it?

Now, I have known most of the answers to these questions for some time. You are right to ask, if that's the case, why haven't I shared them more widely before now? Well, I am a self-effacing, fairly modest kind of guy and I shy away from anything that might remotely look like bragging. I am also well aware that the wheels can come off the bus of our lives at any time. However, it was put to me that I might not be the only person on the planet who thinks that life has to be tough.

What if others wanted to live a charmed and magical life too, but didn't know how or where to start? What if we didn't have to go to hell and back to reach enlightenment? What if, by telling my story, I could help introduce a new magic for a new era?

| money |

MONEY DOES NOT EXIST. THIS IS WHY SO MANY PEOPLE HAVE TROUBLE MAKING IT APPEAR IN THEIR LIVES.

If you look at Earth from Space, even the most sensitive probe cannot detect the presence of money. These days, most of it even exists as a set of ones and zeroes inside computer systems. Recently, Bitcoins have even arrived as a purely virtual currency. Animals and plants also get along fine without any cash. It is just we humans that give it any attention or importance.

Money is often demonised as being the root of all evil. This is a shame, as the ethos behind it has allowed our modern society to evolve to its current state.

Before we look at the good things that money has brought our way, I should share that I don't have loads of money but I do have enough of it. I am certainly not rich, but I am also certainly not poor.

From when I first started employment, I have pretty much always had just enough money to do what I want at any time.

I should also share that this is only the first chapter, because many people use the lack of money for an excuse not to do things. Each of the other chapters in this book are equally important when it comes to bringing just enough money your way, just when you need it. When it comes to practical confirmation that your magic is working, you can use the flow of money coming your way as a barometer of how well everything is working.

There is one important maxim that we must bear in mind when invoking all kinds of magic. If we ignore it, the magic will unravel as soon as it is woven.

"Nothing real can be destroyed. Nothing unreal can persist."

The observant reader will immediately see why money can be so elusive as it falls into the 'nothing unreal' bracket.

A BRIEF HISTORY OF CASH

The concept of money is pretty neat. Over the last few thousand years, it has allowed us humans to specialise. Before money existed, trade was primarily carried out by barter. Some trade was, and still is, just pure theft – often accompanied with force and effected by violence.

With barter, if we want something, we just have to swap something we either don't need, or have a surplus of, with someone who has something we do want. So a farmer's crop might buy some animal skins to keep him warm in winter.

The farmer could, of course, keep all his produce for himself and go out and kill that animal, and make his own skin. The problem with this might be that while he is out hunting, someone could come along and steal his crop.

The farmer also has to make sure his crop doesn't perish, by finding enough people who want it just at the perfect time it is ready for consumption. He also has to find enough things he wants to receive in exchange. If the people who want his crops don't wander right past his farm, he will have to go to a market to sell them. Again, this might leave his farm open to attack while he is away.

The introduction of money, and the supply chain, provided the answer. One of the earliest examples of what looks like money dates back 12,000 BCE, in the form of obsidian, used by Anatolian traders in modern-day Turkey. The Babylonians and Phoenicians used livestock and grain as a currency.

What we would recognise as coins today, have been traced back to 750 BCE. Mostly, they were made of precious metals, which had an intrinsic value if melted down.

Gold could be used for jewellery, tin to make receptacles, and harder metals to make swords and arrow tips.

This form of money meant the farmer could sell his crop to an intermediary or trader in exchange for some coins. The trader would then sell the crop on with a mark-up or profit. The farmer could then go and buy his animal skins, and the like, with the coins he had amassed. Barter was also used in parallel and, of course, exists today.

Having a pile of money did bring in some new problems. For starters, it could be stolen. It also wasn't accruing or doing anything sitting around in a pile. Here's where the next great invention came in – the banker or trusted third party.

Banks had secure, guarded vaults, which meant money could be kept relatively safely. They would also loan money to people who needed it, making an interest charge. Some of this interest could be passed back to the original owner of the money so that their stockpile worked for them. Like all things, especially when money is involved, systems were prone to abuse. The tax man also wanted his share of the profits. Around 300 years ago, another innovation came along in the form of the promissory note.

Unlike gold and silver coins, they had no intrinsic value. In the UK today, such bank notes are emblazoned with the words, "I promise to pay the bearer".

Bank notes meant money could be printed cheaply and even created when it didn't really exist. They were also something that could be forged.

Now, I am not an economist, so I don't plan to explore or pontificate on the rights and wrongs of the modern banking and finance industries. I do, however, find it bizarre that a whole industry has arisen which just deals with money. Some of the richest people around don't actually make anything, but just move money around the system.

It is also a bit strange that if you add up the bank accounts and assets of everyone on the planet, at current market values, apparently what we owe each other is around ten or more times all the things we own. Remember that nothing unreal can be preserved.

Nowadays, in modern societies, you can go about your days with no coins or note at all, but just using credit and debit cards to pay for things. They still work on a system of promises. The credit card company promises to pay the trader. You promise to pay the credit card company a month or so later. If you default on your payment, they will enforce their promise, or threat, to charge you more and more money on your debt until you clear it.

Again, I am not passing judgement on what is wrong or right. Our society works like this. All I will say is that I always pay my credit card bills on time and in full.

When we understand that money is no more than a promise, we can shift our thinking completely, and this is where the new magic comes in.

THE PROMISE

When we are born, we have none of what we can call our own money. That is, unless you are born into a wealthy lineage. So, everything in your bank account right now, be it in the red or the black, is a result of promises you have made, kept, or broken.

If you had a job, you promised to turn up on time and undertake some tasks. In return, your employer promised to pay you some money. Sometimes we get paid in advance and sometimes in arrears. This just alters who is promising what first. If you are paid in arrears, do some work, and your employer runs out of money or doesn't like your work, they might renege on their promise. If you are paid in advance and don't show up, physically or mentally, you have not delivered on your promise.

Some unemployed people promise that they are looking for a job, and the government (which is all of us in democratic countries) promise to pay them some money to tide them over.

This arrangement is great for people who need a helping hand, but ultimately unfulfilling for both parties when a desire to work is lacking.

These are all examples again of how things that aren't real can't be preserved. Remember that money cannot be seen from outer space.

In all these transactions, the only thing that is real are the promises. So we promise to turn up for work. Employers promise to pay us. Customers promise to pay the employer for our services or their product. We get some money and buy some things with notes that bear a promise that the vendor will also get paid. Money is just a by-product that oils the wheels of commerce.

If you are self-employed, just skip out the employer step. You promise to deliver a service or a product, and customers give you promissory notes in return.

The word 'promise' is both a noun and a verb. The dictionary definitions give us some clues about how we can deliver promises, which will result in money flowing our way.

DEFINITION OF PROMISE
1. a statement that something will be done or delivered
2. an assurance of what may be expected
3. an indication of future achievement
4. to undertake an agreed task or deliverable
5. to promise some assistance or a gift
6. to promise something will occur at a certain time
7. to show potential

Collectively, these definitions provide the basis upon which we can invoke magic to manifest more money in our world. The key lies in focussing on what we are promising and in trusting all the money we need, and more if we feel we need it, will flow our way as a result.

Let me state that explicitly again.

Focus solely on what you promise to deliver.
Trust that all the money you need will come your way.

When invoking magic, there are some caveats we must bear in mind, which will be covered in more detail later.

For now though, just bear in mind that any magic we use for our benefit is fine so long as its invocation is not to the detriment of others.

BREADCRUMB: To make money appear just when you need it, write yourself a promissory note for the amount of money you would like to receive, and date it when you would like it to come along.

MY PROMISE

So, I mentioned in the introduction that I would be sharing my story by way of example. I must reiterate that my aim is not to brag, but to show that life doesn't have to be hard when we are seeking enlightenment. I should also state that my way is not the only way, and forging your own path is part of the game.

I was raised as one of seven children to working class, Irish Catholic parents in the Moss Side district of Manchester, in Northwest England. My parents chose to have lots of kids and, as a result, we were what you might call relatively poor, but only in some respects.

I don't remember going hungry, but I do remember being embarrassed about living in what was seen as a slum, even back in those days. When I went to grammar school and mingled with children from middle-class backgrounds, this made the embarrassment worse. I used to get off the bus a couple of stops early so my fellow pupils didn't know where I lived.

While my parents left school at the end of World War II without going to higher education, somehow they raised some pretty-bright kids. We all passed exams to get us into grammar schools, and most of us went on to university and clawed our way into what, these days, you might call the middle classes. I guess we would be called baby boomers.

So, I showed my 'promise' from an early age. I did my eleven-plus exams at the age of nine, took my O Levels (GCSEs nowadays) at fifteen, and A Levels at seventeen. I was a bright kid, as were my siblings. The rivalry helped, as did the mutual teaching and mentoring. My elder brother helped me with homework, and I helped my younger brothers and sister in turn.

Instead of going to University at age seventeen, I took a year off and started working. Bizarrely, my first job was in the Unemployment Offices. I went to register for work and they liked me so much that I was back there the next week calculating benefits for the unemployed. Even then, in 1976, I found it horrific that whole families knew no other way to get money but to sign on. Children of parents on 'the dole' would think it was normal to be on benefits, and that it was crazy to contemplate actually doing any work.

This life was not for me: I had aspirations. The magic of electronics – or electrickery, as I call it nowadays – fascinated me, and I took a degree learning how it all worked. Unlike many of my fellow students, I had a positive bank account containing money I had earned and not been given. Indeed, from the age of seventeen, I paid rent to my parents. I later bought them a house they lived in rent-free until they passed away.

I loved University and the freedom it brought my way, living away from home for the first time. I enjoyed it more because I had cash to enjoy myself.

In my final year, I specialised in television technology and had been offered two jobs before graduating – one at the BBC, and one with ITV as it was then. I took the BBC job as it offered more money, and got a job being paid to have fun playing with cutting-edge technology.

My promise blossomed even more at this stage. I was really good at what I did. Cameramen would come to me and ask if I could add 'go faster stripes' to their cameras in the form of additional functionality. The BBC gave me an award for innovation for one of my inventions. After just two years, I got a job with Sony as their camera expert and they doubled my BBC salary.

Within another two years, a company in London headhunted me and doubled my salary again. They wanted me on board so much that my 'interview' with them was a real treat, watching them at work recording a David Bowie concert in Holland.

By this time, I'd kind of lost track of what was in the bank as my promise of what I was delivering accrued more and more bank notes.

Before I knew it, I cut ties with this company and formed my own specialist engineering consultancy. I then had employees promising me to work hard in exchange for salaries I paid them. As I expanded, I hit some hard times, and sometimes kept my promise to pay them on months I failed in my promise to pay myself.

In 1990, I reached the age of thirty-two, and the world went into recession. This was a recession I somehow rode out through sheer innovation and inventiveness. I ended up with several patents to my name and eventually sold my first business for a nice package.

This pattern repeated itself for the next fifteen years, with two other business ventures, one in CCTV and one in ecommerce, until I was in my mid-forties. Life was okay, and some great things happened, as you will learn, but I was a bit burned out and disillusioned. Having achieved so much, I wondered if there was more to life than this. Little did I know what was coming my way. The potential of my current promises was incredible.

When I look back now, I can see I primarily made two types of promise. I promised to turn up for work, to work really hard, and to impress my employers. They rewarded me royally for this and that is why I got headhunted so much. I also promised customers, in exchange for their promise of cash, that I could help them make some money.

I made their cameras look great, and designed widgets that made their life easier. All of this made them more employable. They were throwing money at me.

Back then, my resource was detailed knowledge of how electrickery worked. These days, I have been exploring the mind and its potential.

As a result, my promises today exist in the form of books like this, audio visualisations, and teaching materials that help expand what we humans are capable of. The vast majority of these 'products' can be delivered without any intervention from me, making the potential revenue huge. In turn, people who consume these materials can unleash untapped and unlimited potential in themselves and others. This provides a multiplier effect, which is near infinite when we think in cosmic terms.

When we create the right promise, it allows money energy to flow our way and we can then go around the circle once again. I am poised at the next revolution.

THE CATCH

You would be right to ask why, with all this promise, that I am not a billionaire. I have asked myself the exact same question.

Well, the realisation of my current promise has only just come about by actually writing this chapter. For the last ten years, while developing all this potential, I have never earned so little.

At the same time, I have not wanted for anything either or been happier. I live in a beautiful house, without a mortgage, in a beautiful part of the country, with a beautiful wife.

All the money I ever need just seems to turn up just when I need it. If I did need any more surplus, by way of balance that money energy has to have somewhere to flow, otherwise it will fester and stagnate.

This is why if you look at my website, (at the time of writing), you will find I am giving free access to several of my eLearning resources, philanthropically, to people with certain types of dis-eases.

YOUR PROMISE

If you are reading this chapter at all, it is probably because you would like some more money in your life.

For more money to come your way, all you have to do is look at what you are currently promising to do.

If you are in a job, do you enjoy it and give it your all? If not, what can you change so you would love it and thrive and prosper there?

Could you acquire new skills and deliver more promise? This might get you a promotion or allow you to find a new job that you do love where you get paid more.

If you are self-employed and don't earn as much as you'd like, there are even more options open to you.

You can change your hourly or daily rate. If you don't think you are worth it, what else can you promise to deliver that would add more value?

Do you have knowledge or expertise that can be delivered virtually? In which case, there has never been a better time to write and publish that book.

There are myriads of places on the Interweb where you can host text, audio and video teaching, and transmutational and healing resources.

Just look at the companion assets that accompany this book for inspiration.

There is no better feeling than waking up to find someone has sent you some money in exchange for one of your promises while you were sleeping.

If you do want to charge more for your services, you can always bundle these virtual products to create more added value.

By the way, if you are currently unemployed and short of cash, there is no end of free or inexpensive teaching resources available on the Interweb. Whether you want to learn a language, play an instrument, or fold origami shapes, there is no excuse for not augmenting what you can do these days.

Make yourself one promise and it will bring more riches your way. Just learn something new each day.

| time |

LIKE THE LACK OF MONEY, THE LACK OF TIME IS PERHAPS THE NEXT BIGGEST EXCUSE FOR US NOT ACHIEVING OUR DREAMS. THE TWO, OF COURSE, ARE INTERLINKED.

I've lost count of the times people have told me that they haven't had time to take my time management programme when, ironically, the time spent taking it will potentially come back to them in spades.

Investment of time is similar in some ways to how we might invest and spend money energy, as we can use our time wisely to make and save even more time. A good example of this is creating a book, or an eCourse, one that can be absorbed by many more people than you could ever deliver to face to face.

It might be somewhat ironic, but we spend little time thinking about time and how we use it. The world has gone 24/7, yet we don't give a second thought as to why there are only 24 hours in each day.

These days, so many people seem to be afflicted by a kind of temporal malaise, where they constantly complain that there is not enough time and that they could use an eighth day in their week.

We are indoctrinated with the notion of time from birth. Babies have times for feeding, changing, and bathing. Our school lessons are regulated by timetables. School-time all too quickly morphs into the nine-to-five of work-time. We intersperse our days with breakfast times, break times, lunch times, tea times, and supper times. Commuters just have to catch that train right on time.

We have a bedtime and, before we know it, it's time to get up again. Note that between these two times, when we are sleeping and dreaming, time takes on a different and ethereal quality. If you ever end up awake in the small hours however, time can seem to stretch to eternity.

Our language, too, is littered with temporal references:

"Just a minute."

"Give me a second."

"Cometh the hour, cometh the man."

"Clocking in late; clocking off early."

"That is so last season."

"Holding back the years."

Time is imposed upon us from birth right through to death and we cannot escape either its forward arrow or its grip.

In our so-called modern society, what is making this somewhat worse is that the world is permanently 'switched on'. Before we had electric light, people snuffed out candles and went to sleep when it was dark.

STOP THE WORLD I WANT TO GET OFF

When I was born, in the late 1950's, the UK had just the two TV channels. Neither transmitted programmes after midnight, and they started up when people came home from work. By the time I graduated from university and got my dream job as an engineer at the BBC at the end of the 70's, TV came in glorious Technicolor, and satellite TV had literally lifted off.

Wind the clock on by just a few decades to today, and we are now overloaded with information. In the UK alone, our four terrestrial TV channels have morphed into hundreds of digital channels. Some of them repeat themselves an hour later. Many of them can be tapped into 'on demand'.

Unless you are at the bottom of a gold mine, every minute of every day, their electromagnetic signals pass through your body unnoticed, along with thousands of radio channels, mobile phone calls, and text messages. It's lucky we aren't tuned into them.

What's more, we have all become broadcasters over the Internet. If you have a smart phone or tablet, you can generate news as it happens, do a funny dance that goes viral, or post a message online to change hearts and minds. YouTube is now one of the most watched 'TV channels' on the planet, and we all generate, curate, and share its content.

These same smart devices are also our windows into this virtual world. The ubiquitous availability of high-speed broadband and mobile data networks means that we are always connected. Each year, more and more of us are generating and consuming more and more data. It is estimated that over two-billion people own a mobile device. They are all Narrowcasters, many people broadcasting to a few.

People even take their phones and that different type of tablet to bed these days. Many check their email, Facebook page, and Twitter feed before retiring and upon waking. Some enterprising therapists are now making a living by treating people so afflicted with email, computer game, and social media addictions. An unwanted side-effect of social media is that it can somewhat ironically cause us to be antisocial.

Like all human advancements, there are good and not so good ramifications to the growing media mountain. My personal view is that the benefits outweigh any negatives. For example, I was able to research some of the data for this book from the comfort of my sofa, with my iPad.

The manuscript ebbed and flowed to and from my editor via email. The print and ebook files were published by being uploaded to online book stores over the Internet. No manuscript ever got printed out and mailed anywhere at any time.

Many readers of the print version of the book may have sampled it and purchased it without taking time out to go to a book shop. Increasingly, more people just download books on to e-readers, smartphones, and tablets. From the resulting reduction in the burning of fossil fuels alone, this is a good thing. Most importantly of course, it saved me loads of time and allowed the book to come out in not much time at all, compared to publishing methods available only a decade ago.

Some people, though, choose to spend their days looking down, and out of what we call reality into a virtual world. This man-made netherworld is populated with Angry Birds, Crushed Candy, trolls, spammers, and 'bots, and has some nasty viruses floating around to infect those with weak defences.

Like all tools, the Internet can be used to save time or waste time. It should be our slave, and we can choose not to be enslaved by it. Likewise, we can turn the TV off at any time, use it to turn our minds off, or use it for education or entertainment. The choices are ours. When we are mindful about how we utilise our time, we can find that there are actually enough hours in the day. We created time so we can uncreate it and redefine it.

It is then that we discover, too, an easier and smarter way to go about our days, where external events seem to happen at just the right time.

The secret to living such a charmed existence lies in taking control of your Personal Time Machine – your mind – or, more specifically, your minds.

People who live a time-full existence are super-productive, super-creative, and also super-lucky. They always land on their feet. For them, the glass isn't so much half-full but positively overflowing. As a result, they not only seem to have time to get all they want done, but seem to have an amazing capacity to help others as well.

While being time-full is an initiative we undertake from an individual and personal perspective, it is scalable and has commercial applications too. When whole departments and businesses work time-fully, they get more done than their competitors and in less time.

They take action more quickly and are always faster out of the block as they are more reactive to market conditions and opportunities. They spend less time in meetings, so they can then spend more time creating products and services or out selling or delivering them to customers. Their employees are happier too and are less prone to take days off with illness and to change jobs.

THE KEY TO LIVING TIMEFULLY

So what are the keys to living such a life?

It lies in understanding how the perception of the passage of time is created by where and how we direct our attention. If we lose focus from the task in hand, then our efficiency drops. By using simple mindfulness techniques, our minds can become immune from the distractions and bandits of time that are sent to plague us. When we live a timeful existence, we are able to jump outside linear time and tasks seem to get done within the time we have allocated to them.

This has some amazing spin offs as it reduces stress and improves health and vitality. In turn, this increases overall productivity and leads to higher creative output. On the surface, this feat might be seen as if it's magic but there are no arcane secrets here, and no sleight-of-mind. This book contains simple and practical techniques that can be learned by everyone, with ease. Remember, at all times, any magic trick ceases to be magic once we know how it's done.

Maybe you've seen and admired those people who seem to get so much done, and wondered how they pack it into their days. Perhaps they are insomniacs and never sleep. Maybe they have a 25th hour secreted away somewhere in each of their days.

"Give it to a busy person," they say.

Although time does tick relentlessly forwards, remarkably it is both malleable and stretchable. We have all experienced this phenomenon.

If you have a busy day at the office, the hours can fly by and, before you know it, you ask where the time went. If you are waiting for the phone to ring, perhaps when a customer promised to call with a sales order, minutes can stretch into hours. The perceived passage of time is subjective.

The reason for this seeming paradox is that the nature and content of our thoughts, and the state of our consciousness, have an effect on how we experience time. By using simple and repeatable mindfulness techniques, we can manipulate time to our advantage. When we learn to change our mind, we change our time.

What's even better still, is that taking such a mindful approach to managing our time brings many collateral benefits. As well as being able to achieve more high-quality output in less time, we become more healthy, vibrant, lucky, and 'attractive'.

Many studies also indicate that adoption of mindfulness techniques increases our longevity. If true, the sooner we start, the more we may potentially benefit over our whole lifetime. If we can live longer, it makes sense that we also enjoy a good quality of life for any additional years we might generate. The key to doing this is to learn to meditate.

The very thought of this can put many people off. There is no need to sit cross-legged in a darkened cave chanting "Omm". We are all natural meditators. If you have ever driven anywhere and not remembered how you got from A to B, you had almost certainly entered a low-level meditative state.

Don't think for a minute that this is about joining some strange cult. The techniques I advocate are aimed at dramatically increasing creativity and productivity in real-world business environments. I like to think of it as mindfulness with go-faster stripes, where the going faster somewhat paradoxically requires us to go a little slower.

To many people though, the thought of having unlimited time might cause a problem. The lack of time is the perfect excuse for not getting things done. Some people might even fear their positions would be under threat. Others may be concerned that there would be nothing left to strive for if their dreams were fulfilled.

So, if there was a magical way of generating more time, there would be no let off and no way out. Our To Do list would have to get done!

The answer to any potential overwhelm is not necessarily to throw all this technology, and our clocks, out of the window. That said, some parents and teachers may well want to impose 'device-free' time zones.

In Las Vegas, you will find that casinos have no clocks at all, as they love to keep their gamblers in the dark as to what time it is so that they spend more money.

The first stage in adopting a 'mind-full' approach to time management is to understand how we can so easily fritter away our time mindlessly. It is then that we can start to bring it under our control.

In any world where more time is available, enjoying ourselves and relaxing should be high on the agenda. If we want employees working at their peak, they will need some high quality 'down-time' in order to avoid burn out. Happy employees lead to happy customers, which in turn leads to profitability. By understanding how we perceive the passage of time, it can become our slave, servant, and ally, as opposed to being our tyrant and master. We can learn to utilise time to our advantage, to go with its natural flow, and to stop attempting to push it back up its temporal hill.

The term mindfulness itself can sometimes be used misleadingly by becoming synonymous with meditation. While integrating a meditative practice into our days is a vital component, they are not one and the same thing. In deep meditation, our mind empties itself of the normal internal chatter and enters a time-less place. Somewhat ironically, we could even describe this as being a state of 'mind-less-ness'.

The transformation to a mindful approach to managing our time is somewhat more fundamental and subtle than this.

The normal human mind is only capable of experiencing one thought at a time. If we think about the content of a thought, we lose its direction. If we think about the direction of a thought, we lose its content. Just read those two sentences again and think about them to verify this for yourself.

Note, of course, that there is nothing normal about the human mind. As far as we know, it's the only bit of self-aware matter in the Universe. It's also capable of reprogramming itself in an instant. This is known as neuroplasticity. Note too that nothing about the mind is fixed, and even the singular nature of a thought is not a given.

With this strange ability to only think one thought at a time, if our mind wanders away from the task we are focusing on, our efficiency will drop. This basic aspect of our consciousness leads us to the real reason we become inefficient. When our mind drifts as it is prone and hardwired to do, our productivity drops accordingly.

To add to all of this, there are all those pesky interruptions, diversions, and distractions. In an eight-hour working day, we are often lucky to get an hour of quality creative time.

So think about your thoughts in a typical day. Some of them will be mulling over past events. Perhaps you'll think about conversations that could have gone better. If someone crossed your boundaries, you can spend hours agonising about it. You might of course be harking back to pleasant times like an enjoyable meal, a fabulous holiday, or how you met the love of your life. Alternatively, you may be planning and rehearsing a speech or conversation for a day or more ahead. You may be thinking of what to cook for supper, or longing for the weekend to arrive more quickly and for the working week to finish.

With such a jumble of thoughts running around in a person's head, it is amazing anything gets done. If these thoughts wander into feeling unloved or undervalued, efficiency drops through the floor.

It is clear that intelligent time management involves thought management. When we harness our thoughts, we begin to take time under our control. Timefulness is the new mindfulness.

BREADCRUMB: *Nothing in nature beats to the second other than the thoughts of someone watching the clock.*

ME-TIME

For as far back as I remember, I noticed that people seemed to think at different speeds. I mentioned I was a bright child and I found I picked things up really quickly. I would always zoom ahead to the next part of a lesson ... sometimes to a teacher's annoyance. I sensed that not everyone was wired the same.

When I started my own business, I really began to experience light-bulb moments. These were flashes of brilliance where I saw the whole picture in less than a second. I had one of these just as the recession of the nineties took hold. I didn't know at the time, but it saved my business and allowed us to trade through pretty much unscathed.

One problem that TV cameras had, was that when they pointed at computer screens, they would flicker. At that time, image sensors were changing from tubes to solid-state CCD.

I had a vision one day where I realised I could change the refresh rate of the chip so it synced with the computer screen, and in so doing, get rid of the annoying disturbance. This led to an invention that sold to broadcasters worldwide and made my name as a 'bright young thing'. I even won a Royal Television Society award for my inventiveness – twice!

My relationship with time was pretty much the same as that for everyone else, apart perhaps from being able to think and pick up new concepts rather quickly. That was until I was introduced to meditation in my mid-forties.

Now I reflect back, I realise that all my books touch on temporal themes. I also wrote most of them in what seemed to be 'no time at all'.

My first book, 100 Years of Ermintrude, was written on a plane journey and tells in snapshots of a woman who lives her life backwards. My next book, Blocks, explores how we waste time when we procrastinate. The Art and Science of Light Bulb Moments describes how we jump outside space and time for a moment when we have a flash of inspiration.

The next two books were quite esoteric. Flavours of Thought explores how not all our mind-centres, in and outside our bodies, run to the same time-clock. Planes of Being describes how we are multidimensional beings having an incarnate experience in three-dimensional space, with a forward arrow of time.

The Zone is a delightful exploration of how to get into that magical space where we are in flow. The next two books, This We Know, and This We Are, are a great example of being in flow, as they were both written and published within a month. In both these books, I channelled a possible future for humanity in 100 and 200 year's time. Some of this has already come to pass.

While writing all these books, I experienced time jumps, time replays, and even levitation – which I learned happens when time stops. I also spontaneously developed the ability to see through time by seeing past and future lives in peoples' auras. In addition, I learned to heal by 'softening' time, and also began to teach how to do all of this.

One practical output from all these experiences was the creation of what I understand is the world's first time management programme based on mindfulness, called Living Timefully.

THE CATCH

With this ability to see through time, you would be right to ask why I don't get the lottery numbers for next weekend.

Well, there is an interesting paradox I must share with you. We live in what is known as 'The Duality' where everything we do and experience is preordained, while at the same time, we have the free will to change absolutely everything. While inside the illusion we call reality, it is difficult to understand why these two conditions hold true together.

The upshot is that you can only get the lottery numbers if you are already predestined to win.

YOU-TIME

So, just imagine that there is all the time in the world – what do you need more time for?

What would and could you do if there were enough hours in the day? What excuses would you have to let go?

Answering these questions, is the first step in taking time under your control. When we lose the notion that time is fixed and linear, it bends and stretches so that things just get done at the perfect time. The perfect opportunities and connections also percolate into our world, just when we need them. Life becomes a breeze when we think of things arriving as opposed to us having to turn up.

Somewhat bizarrely, the key to getting to this blissful state is to 'waste' at least ten to thirty minutes every day doing nothing. The practice of daily meditation is the simplest way to bring magic into our lives. It is then that we learn that thoughts don't become things because they are things.

| thought |

DESPERATION, CAUSED BY LACK OF MONEY AND THE IDEA THAT THERE ISN'T ENOUGH TIME, ARE JUST THOUGHTS.

When we're asleep, we don't think them. Before we became self-aware, at the age of seven or so, we didn't think them either. Indeed, most people tend to think they are immortal until they reach their twenties, unless they are unfortunate enough to have an accident or serious illness.

We should be mindful that the thought that the amount of money we have is linked to our promise is also just a thought. The notion that time might be stretchable and that its flow is controllable are just thoughts too.

For most of us, our thoughts fire up upon awakening and only go quiescent when we fall asleep. Most of us don't give our thoughts a second thought during the day. This is a shame, because it is exactly the nature and content of our thoughts that dictate how our days go.

When we reflect on the day just gone, our thoughts tell us how it went. When we think about tomorrow, it is these thoughts that largely dictate how it will unfold. So, getting our thoughts in order is obviously pretty important if, for example, we would like more money in our lives and more time in which to spend it.

It is perhaps somewhat ironic then that the key to marshalling our thoughts lies in learning to meditate. Specifically, it involves learning to enter the meditative state with our eyes open. Both activities at first might seem a waste of time.

NOW HERE'S A THOUGHT

When we think about thought, it is clear that the ability to speak and the ability to run 'self-talk' in our heads are somewhat connected. This is why babies don't 'think' in quite the same way as toddlers, and toddlers in the same way as most adults. In passing, I should mention that we also 'think' in images, music, sounds, smells, tastes, and feelings – both emotional and tactile. We might 'think' for example that a surface of a table is a bit rough, or that a bakery smells nice, without any words passing through our mind.

Our jumble of thoughts is exactly that. What we think from one minute to the next is completely altered by the world around us. We can be having a fabulous day only for a customer to call with a complaint. Whatever we were planning to think about then gets replaced by the thought of that conversation going around and around in our heads. We might be upset that we caused them grief or annoyed at them because they were unjustified in their complaint. Just one incident of this nature can completely ruin our day and stop any thoughts of creativity in their tracks.

When an unwanted thought form of this nature goes around and around in our heads, I call it a 'mindfall'. The reason for such looping cascades is a peculiar nature of thought that we rarely think about, and it is this. The normal human mind is only capable of having one thought at a time, particularly where the thought is one involving an internal dialogue or self-talk. In the same way that we cannot say two things out loud, we can't hold more than one thought 'in loud'. Another way of imagining this is that if we think of the content of a thought, we lose its direction and if we think about its direction, we lose its content. Just pause for a moment to reflect on that.

While you did pause for a moment, you may notice that when you are reading (or writing), you cannot think about something else either. Now there's a thought.

Just to get you thinking a bit more about thoughts, I should share with you something I learned from a shaman (or specifically a shamanka). She told me that most thoughts aren't necessarily what we think of as our own. Now that statement really got me thinking and caused me to research what the sages and mystics thought about thought, whilst also looking into the mind and what neuroscientists were also thinking.

From a scientific perspective, our self-awareness is referred to as one of the 'hard questions'. This is a nice and neat way of saying nobody has the slightest clue about how we are really able to think. Apparently, the atoms we consist of are the remnants of stellar explosions billions of years ago. This makes us sentient and self-aware stardust. Some neuroscientists are coming to the same conclusion about thought, though that has been known intuitively for thousands, if not hundreds of thousands, of years.

More open-minded scientists are speculating that our brains are not just generators of thought but also receivers of thought. If you ever heard a phone ring only to 'know' a second or two before who was on the other end, you will have experienced this phenomenon. More specifically and accurately, our brains are the processing units that receive and replay all thought forms. Our whole neurology is both a receiver and broadcaster.

Thought forms too are not just the words that mill around in our head, the central processing unit. We can receive and transmit what are colloquially referred to as 'vibes'. Our gut centre picks up on the safety of a situation or the advisability on taking a course of action. Our heart centre can quite literally feel the love in a room, or an antipathy. At the same time, we can radiate out our fear and trepidation and whether we like or dislike someone or something.

Remarkably too, the mind centres outside our brains seem to operate a few seconds ahead of our conscious mind. If you have ever regretted not trusting your gut or following your heart, you will have experienced that they are somewhat wiser than our brains. This is perhaps no surprise, as from an evolutionary perspective, they are somewhat older by several million years as it turns out.

The Big Picture of where our thoughts emanate from, and go to, is stranger still. It seems that we are all connected by a collective field of consciousness. This was popularised by people like Jung and, more recently, championed by scientists like Ervin Laszlo and the wonderfully maverick Rupert Sheldrake. Some scientists resist this notion, but I predict by the end of this century, it will be not only embraced but also form the basis of a new and harmonised 'Theory of Everything'. The so-called missing Dark Matter and Dark Energy are aspects of the consciousness field of the universe. It is this field that not only 'holds' the physical universe together but connects everything in it to everything else. This holds across both space and time.

Our neurology receives information from this field and 'uploads' what we are thinking, experiencing, and generating to it. All memories and thoughts from the past, present, and future are stored in this field from all life forms, both conscious and unconscious. Such 'consciousness' is not restricted to plants, insects, or animals.

For example, crystals are rocks with enhanced 'awareness', and snowflakes have more 'sense' than a drop of water. Stars and planets have 'feelings' and 'sensibilities' too. We have just lost, or have yet to find, the ability to tune into them.

So when a thought 'comes in' against the run of our internal dialogue, like a flash of inspiration or a long lost memory, it's an example of us tapping into this field. I like to think of lightbulb moments as being 'future memories' leaking back in time from the Future to the Now. In all cases, if true, it pays great dividends to pay attention to them and to act upon them.

By the way, if you think I have lost my marbles and am taking something hallucinatory, just ask your gut if any of this makes intuitive sense. I have first-hand experience of altered states of awareness that have brought me to this conclusion, and I, for one, am happy for science to catch up. Metaphysics has always been tomorrow's physics after all.

While this complexity might make the world of thoughts completely inaccessible and bewildering, it actually leads us to a place where we can begin to unravel our thoughts and make our thought forms have an influence in our physical world. When it comes to generating money and time, you can start to see why we must get our thoughts, like ducks, in a row.

STOP MY MIND I WANT TO GET OUT

Now, unravelling our thoughts is a bit like repairing an engine in car while travelling at speed, but from the passenger compartment. We naturally would take the car into a garage, open the bonnet, and then begin our analysis.

This is why, when it comes to getting our thoughts under control, the best way by far is to meditate. Most meditation uses either the breath or a mantra (or sound) to give our thoughts a focus. Remember, when we think of something else, like the in and out breath, this can result in our thoughts going quiet. This is why such meditations are so useful if we are disturbed, anxious, or stressed as they help quell our inner demons and get our so-called 'Monkey Mind' to shut up.

There is a slightly more advanced technique where we meditate on thought itself, which leads to us completely changing our relationship with the ramblings and ruminations of our mind. In this mode, when a thought comes in, we can ask it where it came from and for what purpose. If it's a thought we don't want in our head, we can then ask it to turn around and go away. If it is a useful thought, we can ask it for more information about why it turned up and why at this particular time.

Now, I will be the first to admit that this technique might sound like a flight of imagination. It is, however, a method whereby we actively encourage and promote imagination. For example, I meditate before writing this and every chapter. Before starting the meditation, I will of course know the rough subject matter and what I want the chapter to be about, but I might not have the start, the end, and the flow that takes me there. Normally, five or so minutes in, I get the first sentence and then I wait as long as I can before I can't hold any more of the chapter. I open my eyes and let it flow.

I then remain in the meditative state while writing and it is almost like the chapter is 'read out' to me before my eyes. After doing this 'by accident' for a few years, I learned that this is what people call 'channelling'. This is something I now unexpectedly find myself teaching others. Such 'channellings' are not restricted to words on a page. Actors talk about channelling a character in a play or film. Musicians 'channel' each other. I even learned how to ghost-write for other authors, and was told that the words I generated sounded more like them than them.

These are all examples of what happens when we tune in to the collective consciousness. It is nothing weird. Some people claim they are channelling angels, archangels, or aliens. I have worked with others who channel animals and some who commune with fairies at the bottom of the garden. My personal belief is that we tune into a future version of ourselves who knows the words we have yet to write. We can call it our Creative Muse. I am not so worried about the actual mechanism. To me, it is the output we generate from such techniques that is of more importance. All my books, including this one, were written this way, and you can judge its efficacy.

There is some misunderstanding that meditation is about cancelling out and annulling all thought. Thought is very much allowed and encouraged, but what meditation helps with is the reduction of repetitive thoughts that won't go away. This doesn't have to be thoughts of remorse, self-loathing, or anger. It might be a speech you are preparing or a conversation with your boss that you are dreading.

Like all things, the more you practice, the better quality of creative output you can produce. At the same time, there are numerous benefits to be had in stress reduction and improved wellbeing. What is perhaps less recognised is how meditation helps change our luck. We seem to attract just what we need, just when we need it. There are several mechanisms in operation here.

The first is that we are calmer and people are attracted to us. Secondly, as our minds are less busy, we leave space and time to notice just what can help us. Lastly, it is conjectured that we radiate out thought forms into the collective, and then conjure up what looks like magic in our lives. Again, the mechanism is somewhat academic as it is the result that counts. All we have to bear in mind is that the mind-calming effect of regular meditation is essential if we want to become masterful at manifestation. Loose thought forms will generate undesirable effects in our lives.

FLAVOURS OF THOUGHT

Adoption of a daily meditative practice costs nothing, other than a little time. My personal experience is that days when I don't meditate just don't go as well, so I counterintuitively waste time by not spending that little time. If I don't get ten or twenty minutes spare, I have learned to meditate when walking the dogs or even while commuting on a busy train.

I noticed something else occurring after a year or so. I started to be able to differentiate between the 'tone' of different sources of thought forms. It was, perhaps, no surprise that this happened while writing my book, Flavours of Thought, after I had discovered the magic of the Major Arcana of the Tarot.

Incidentally, I had the light-bulb moment that thoughts come in different flavours when writing my book, The Art and Science of Light Bulb Moments. This is an example of how self-fulfilling our path becomes when we live in the meditative state continually. It is like our path is shown to us and all we have to do is follow it.

I'd already chanced upon a book that explained how the 22 cards of the Major Arcana each related to a different mode of thinking. What's more, it became clear that the ancients 'knew', or intuited, that our thoughts could emanate from either our conscious mind, our unconscious mind-centres, or the collective consciousness.

I also discovered that thought forms could be grouped and typified. There are a group of thought forms that come from the collective consciousness. I called them Ethereal Whispers, as they come in like a wisp of a wind. Other thought forms emanate from our unconscious mind-centres. I called these Unconscious Murmurs, as they are largely silent and often subtle. Then we have Directive Thoughts, which are the more familiar types of thought we have in our head.

Part of the illusion is that it is the Directive Thoughts that 'drive the bus'. Many of them, however, are seeded from an Ethereal Whisper or an Unconscious Murmur, sometimes from both. When we acknowledge where thoughts really come from, a new level of magic comes into our world. To external observers, this makes us even luckier because we start to gain mastery over what manifests in our lives.

To do this, all we have to do is to allow an Ethereal Whisper to seed an Unconscious Murmur and for that to percolate into a Directive 'head-based' thought. In my book, I formed many collections of these patterns and called them recipes. They are, in effect, a kind of modern day spell. Now, many books on personal development often refer the reader to previous or even future books as a place to get their enlightenment. Of course, I'd like to you to read my other books, as there is much magic embedded in them, but let me give you a Master Recipe here that you can use to universally make things happen.

Let's say you'd like a new job or partner, or just a general bit of good fortune to come your way. Take yourself out for a walk alone in nature and look around you.

Firstly, notice what is around you. What's the weather like? What are the colours like? What season are you in? Can you hear or smell anything?

Then zero in on the one thing or things you notice the most. This might be something strange like a broken gate, a flower, or a particular cloud.

Secondly, just let your awareness close in on that thing. You may want to stop and cogitate for a while. You can even ask it if it has a message for you. You can speak to it and let it speak to you. Allow it to tell you about its symbolic nature and how that relates to whatever it is that you desire being missing from your life.

Thirdly, take that message as a metaphor and deduce what it means about you and your life at that particular time. Ask yourself what you can do to change yourself internally so that you no longer attract the 'no-thing'.

When you return home, there is no need to take action right away to set right what you've learned.

Sleep on it, pay attention to your dreams, and the next morning just be different about the way you go about your day.

Be mindful of the old thought pattern related to what you observed and, should it surface, thank it for coming along to remind you and ask it to go away. Then, as if by magic, all you have to do is wait for what you desire to show up.

For those interested in further study, or with a Tarot deck, this 'spell' uses The Moon, The Hermit, and The Emperor. Get those three cards out and leave them around where you see them each day and you will increase the magic. You will find this 'spell' at the very back of this book.

This exercise (and spell) might sound trivial (or farcical), but such interaction with the world around us and the cognisance of the connected nature of all things is the fundamental tenet of all practical magic.

The world around us is a mirror of what is inside – and vice versa. There is only one person responsible for the state of our life and that is us. Period.

BREADCRUMB: *Einstein worked out the Theory of Relativity by imagining he was riding down a beam of light. Just imagine your whole life is you riding down a pre-existing thought stream. Then imagine how you might redirect it, alter the thoughts, and even get off.*

THE CATCH

This brings us to the catch in evoking any magical spell, which also emphasises the need for a calm mind and regular meditation.

It is not just our head that emanates thought forms. So while your head might radiate the desire for something to turn up in your world, your unconscious mind is silently in operation too. It can be emanating the fear that something might not turn up. So both thought forms wander out into the collective and can cancel out and interfere with each other. Of course, if the fear of not having something is greater than the desire to have it, you can guess what shows up.

Our unconscious mind acts as our protector, and can block just what you want in your life as it might unsettle the status quo. Why fix something that is not broken, even though it might not be working perfectly?

So, if we harbour fears, anger, or guilt, this is a great way to bring events that will trigger them into our world. The effect is cyclic.

BEING THOUGHT-FULL

Our thoughts are important, and to live a magical life we need to pay attention to them. Learning to enter the meditative state with our eyes open allows us to see the world with new eyes. Indeed, when we learn to perceive with all our mind-centres, a whole new panoply opens up for us.

Our gut and heart especially like to be listened to. As you will see, they can also be taken under control and used for all manner of magic.

It is time to form a new and thought-full relationship with your thoughts. When they come in, talk to them. Ask them why they came and why they have come along right now. If thought patterns repeat, recognise you are in a mindfall. Meditate on your mindfalls and watch them float away.

Notice the whispers of thoughts on the wind and let them come into your awareness. Listen to the tone and sound of their 'voice' and how they communicate not just with words but in signs, symbols, and serendipities.

| love |

I WORK WITH SO MANY REALLY LOVELY
PEOPLE WHO SEEM TO HAVE THINGS MISSING FROM
THEIR LIVES. ALONGSIDE LACK OF MONEY AND THE
PERCEPTION THAT THERE IS NOT ENOUGH TIME, IT
SEEMS THAT SOME AMAZINGLY BEAUTIFUL PEOPLE
ARE LONELY AND CAN'T SEEM TO FIND THE LOVE OF
THEIR LIFE.

Some have loved and lost and been a bit burned on the
way. Some just don't seem to find Mr or Mrs Right. Some,
of course, just want to be alone, and that's fine too.
Indeed, one ability required for us to fall in love and to be
loved is that we are comfortable in our own skin and
company.

If you listen to the music, love seems to be in the air,
and love is all around. There are no end of 'rom-coms'
where two people get together, some mishap befalls them,
they learn something about themselves and each other,
and end up kissing and making up. The formula seems so
simple yet can be elusive too.

At first, the themes I am writing about in order to create a magical life, might seem somewhat eclectic. By the end of this chapter, I hope you will begin to see that the order of the chapters themselves is not random.

When you realise that money and time are connected to what we think about them, it will come as no surprise that love is a state of mind as well. Two people can look at a work of art and one might loathe it and the other adore it. Beauty is so in the eye of the beholder.

Love is also much more about being in love with someone else and finding the most perfect soul mate. It is equally about being in love with ourselves and who we are, what we do and what values we hold dear and cherish.

Love is also a universal energy, and I don't mean this metaphorically. The force of gravity and love are one and the same thing. The Earth revolves around the Sun because it loves, too.

This bond is strong and billions of years old, and pervades across the whole of space and time. The same love-bond exists between the Moon and the Earth and all the stars revolving around the centre of our galaxy. Cosmologists have even discovered that our galaxy and many others revolve around what they term a Great Attractor.

We may be talking about 'love bonds', which sound at first dissimilar, but the terminology is the same.

I should emphasise that I have not read about this correlation in any book, I just 'channelled' it. I also checked this with another channel I know and she confirmed it to be the way the universe works.

By the way, when I make statements of this nature, I encourage you to both take them with a pinch of salt and also to check in with your gut mind too as to their veracity.

BE, DO, LOVE

So, if we want to attract a person or a life of our dreams, all we have to do is turn the notch up a bit on our personal 'gravitational' field. When we do this, we also tune into matching fields of the perfect soul mates and opportunities.

I love reading the wisdom of Rudolph Steiner. Some of his books are quite complex and, frankly, a bit out there, but I love them nonetheless. What I love in particular is this: He wrote them a century or more ago in German and using phraseology which can be daunting. Yet I have lost count of the times they confirm certain thoughts I have had one-hundred years later, before I even read them.

I have always believed human speech and thought must be interlinked and must also be magical by its very nature. For us to think something and say it out loud, we have to take conscious control over something we are unconscious about – our voice box.

As I move my fingers to type these words, I can see them and how they operate. I have no idea what my voice-box looks like if I speak them.

Our throat is our fifth chakra point and what Steiner points out in his book, Cosmic Memory, is how humans learned to take conscious control of their 5th chakra point several million years ago. He further postulates that we are about to take control of our 4th chakra point, the heart centre.

Chakras, by the way, are vortices that connect our mind centres with the collective mind.

This is the key to being supremely attractive. Discovering how to do it though is somewhat of a work in progress for me, but I do have some clues how to go about it.

The first clue lies in making sure our heart is working optimally and realising that the route to loving someone else means that we have to love ourselves first. This strengthens and attunes our own heart so we can bond it with the heart mind of another.

Now this doesn't mean being in love with ourselves in a narcissistic way. It is vital that we love ourselves if we can ever hope to get someone else to love us truly too.

This means we have to love what we do as much as we must love who we are.

So if you find yourself in that job that you don't like so much, you have a couple of choices that we mentioned in the chapter on money. Either change how you approach and tackle your job so you do love it, or get a new job. The latter especially might require you to up-skill a little.

Outside work, find activities that you also love to do. Ideally, make sure one or two of them aren't solitary as that might just be where you meet your life partner.

After making yourself internally more attractive, the next step is quite practical and that's to work on the external you. So, find some new clothes and ones that you feel most comfortable to wear. If money is an issue, visit a few charity shops or look out for the sales. Get clothes that can mix and match so you can create more outfits. They shouldn't be too tight on your body, unless you have the figure for it, or be too baggy. Dress for the season too.

Then it's time to give yourself a makeover, but staying well shy of cosmetic surgery. Get your hair done. Find a hairdressing college for a free hairdo if money's tight. Treat yourself to a facial. If you can, lose a few pounds. If you find this tricky, you may be surprised how meditation using the diaphragm changes your physiology so that you burn more calories. I love win-wins.

These are simple tasks that operate silently in the background, strengthening the attractivity of your heart centre.

The next step is to start broadcasting. It's time to do something that gets you noticed. This doesn't mean auditioning for Xfactor or Your Country's Got Talent. Show up at local events or, even better, get involved on the organising team. Charities are crying out for willing volunteers to share some of their love with people who need it. Joining a night class is a great way of meeting like-minded souls with a common interest.

If you have an artistic talent, share your flair online. Blog your words, Instagram your photos, Pinterest your art, SoundCloud your music, and YouTube your humour. It is also often overlooked how using our brain burns up calories. It is about 2% of our body weight, but while we are awake and mentally engaged, it uses 25% of our body's fuel. Using your brain and you will burn calories, especially when you are learning something new.

Whatever loving initiatives you choose to adopt, what is important is that put your heart into them and while keeping a weather-eye on your ego.

THE LANGUAGE OF LOVE

The word love comes up pretty much constantly in our culture. You cannot listen to an hour of popular music radio without at least one song being played that has love in the title or at least its lyrics. Put the word love into an Amazon search, and you will find around half-a-million books with love in their titles or content.

Like the word 'nice' though, or 'like' for the younger generation, it can suffer from overuse somewhat. It is important to be mindful of our own use of the word so we only use it when we absolutely mean it. This is a word to be cherished and not one to be diluted.

If people around us hear that we simply love everything, then they will not take us seriously when we really love something or someone. It is wise to be judicious between what we love and what we merely like. This holds true too for the use of the heart emoticon in our text and social media messages.

Words hold and transmit a power through the airwaves similar to thoughts in the field of the collective consciousness. So when we speak, either out loud or 'in loud', use the word love sparingly and when you really mean it.

THE HEART RAY

When you tune in to the aura and learn to perceive it, with sight or feeling, you can see each of our chakra points has a whirling vortex, or rays, associated with it. For our 2nd, 3rd, 4th, 5th, and 6th chakras, they tend to be at ninety degrees to our body, coming out at the front and back. They tend to beam out from the front and receive in from the back. For our 1st and 7th chakras, they point vertically downwards and upwards respectively.

Note that under conscious control, the direction and strength of each vortex can be altered. So, for example, we can point our heart ray downwards and send love to the Earth. We can split our heart ray in two in front of us and loop it around our bodies into our backs. This gives us a little boost of self love which is really useful if we are feeling a bit down or if the world is a little against us.

The heart ray can also be sent into the hearts of people in a potentially fractious meeting, ahead of time, to soften any tension.

When two people fall in love, their heart rays entwine. Like all particles in the universe, this creates entanglement so that, when apart, hearts are still locked together.

All magic can be used for either altruistic or nefarious purposes. So in this book, I have mentioned the existence of the heart ray but I will not explain how to switch it on.

The reason for this is that we must use our heart ray for the purposes of spreading unconditional love.

We could, for example, use it to make someone fall in love with us against their wishes, or at the wrong time. When used to soften tense meetings, our intent should be to help people be generally less angry, and not so the outcome of the meeting turns solely in our favour. You can see that fine balance and a high level of ethics is required when using magic.

Some readers will be attuned already and will be able to tap into it and control it. Others will have to be initiated. If you are ready, you will find a resource to help you.

BREADCRUMB: *What might be the purpose of the rays that emanate from your solar plexus and sacral chakras once they are taken under conscious control? What's the possible use of the rays coming from your third eye and crown and root chakras?*

ALL MY LOVING

When I look back at how I found my life partner, I can see how much loving what I did played such a big part in bringing us together. I'd had a few relationships, mostly to practice at it all I guess, but I knew none were 100% right. I worked at Sony, as their camera expert, and got called out by a company in London to give some TLC to one of their cameras. I had no idea that the person who called to book me was to become my soul mate.

At the time, broadcast TV engineers were mostly males and in their forties and fifties. Imagine my soul mate's surprise when this young, bright eyed, confident, and capable chap turned up, who sorted out a complex technical task, in what seemed no time at all.

After a bit of a shuffle around with our respective, non-ideal current partners, we got together. I remember thinking how much it felt like a hand in a perfectly sized glove. Now she had to get to work quickly on my needs for better clothes, shorter hair, and a bit of moisturiser. My rather naff car got replaced by something rather more sleek and sporty too. Apparently, I brushed up rather well.

Over thirty years later, we find ourselves loving, sharing, and enjoying life together in a rather nice part of the world. Being my soul mate, she is also my best friend and confidant. We are fortunate that we have many of the same likes, and dislikes, so love doing stuff together.

The real key to our relationship is that my soul mate loves me doing the few things I like doing that she doesn't, and I reciprocate in kind.

A relationship like this doesn't just work without some thoughtfulness and 'kindfulness'. It benefits from continual small improvements to make it deepen still further. If I do some shopping or work around the house, I will always go that extra mile and add something on top of what's needed.

We love surprising each other with evenings out or sumptuous and tasty meals in. We mutually agreed not to have children, but our faithful and loving four-legged house mates give us delights on most days at least. People who visit our house report on how loving the space feels.

Some more icing on the cake is that we are fortunate to both run our own businesses in fields we are passionate about.

Like many people our age, in their mid-fifties, we also find ourselves supporting elderly parents and relatives in various stages of health. In some cases, it has been support in transition to the other side. In all instances, love conquers the darkest of days and I feel truly blessed.

That said, I don't for a minute rest on any laurels and take anything for granted. A curved ball can get lobbed our way when we least expect it.

Maintaining the best of health with good food, clean air and, above all, as good a mind as we both can hope to have is high on the agenda.

My aim is that my business of sharing wisdom and teachings of what I have learned across the Internet will keep my mind active for as long as possible. At the same time, it handily generates revenue. I have also found recently that I can use some of this to fund philanthropic initiatives and also to leave a legacy behind long after I return to Source. This has given me something else to be passionate about and to put my soul and heart into.

THE CATCH

Our heart mind is more powerful than our head. Not only can we use it in finding and giving love, but we can use it to heal anyone anywhere on the planet in the past, present and future.

While we learn to take our heart mind under conscious control though, we have to take care and pay due diligence. Our heart can get over-stretched and end up being broken.

Once we learn that the more love we give out, the more we get back, it's tempting to give even more still. We have to be mindful to balance the in flow and out flow so that they are more or less even. If we don't, it can backfire on the giver so that if we get hurt, we turn off the tap in order to protect ourselves.

Fortunately, the universal source of love is infinite, so once the love inflow and outflow is balanced, it tends to stay that way.

CREATING A TO LOVE LIST

There is a simple technique you can use to keep the flow of love nicely in balance. It involves ditching your To Do list and creating and using a To Love list.

We can get somewhat overwhelmed with our To Do lists. Some people have several of them that they just add to, so that they never get any shorter. As a result, like our email InBox, they can get bigger and bigger and become completely unmanageable and unwieldy. Some people even spend so much time curating their To Do lists that they end up not getting anything done.

It's said that when we love the work we do, we'll never work as such again. So just imagine if everything on your To Do list was something you simply loved to do.

Here's how to create a To Love List. You'll need two blank sheets of paper. Label one sheet of paper a To Love List and one a To Don't List.

First, scan all the items on your To Do list, or lists, and transfer the ones you really would rather not do over to the sheet labelled To Don't List, Cross them off your To Do List as you go.

You should now be left with a To Do List with just the things you actually like doing.

So, in the order that you would love to do them first, transfer them to the blank sheet of paper labelled as your To Love list.

Now have a look at your To Don't List. It will probably have things on it that need doing, even if you don't like to do them. See which ones you can outsource or delegate to someone else. Then take action to pass them on.

With the tasks you have left, have a think of how you could tackle them or what would have to change with them so you would love to do them. Then move them across to your To Love List.

At this point, you should be able to rip up the old To Do List and bin the To Don't List.

The next step is easy: just tackle your To Love list from the top down. This way you will only do the things you like doing the most in the order you'd love to do them.

What's not to love about that?

| wellbeing |

THE OBSERVANT READER MIGHT BY NOW HAVE SPOTTED A CERTAIN LOGIC AND FLOW TO THE THEMES OF THE CHAPTERS IN THIS TOME.

I started with a chapter on money solely because the lack of it seems to be high on so many agendas of so many people these days. If we could somehow conjure up some money into our world, what better proof could there be that we should look into this magical world some more?

It is worth pointing out that it's a misconception that money can't buy us more time, love, or even our health.

While it may not exactly buy us more than our allotted time on Earth, it can be used to pay other people to do things to give us more time to do the things we love.

While it can't exactly buy us the love of a soul mate, we can invest it energetically into projects, activities, and people we love. We can love what we do with it.

It is also said that our health and wellbeing is something money can't buy. Well, this is not exactly true either. In the First World at least, it pays for our healthcare and sanitation, and our food and water. If you have a roof over your head to keep out the elements, it pays for that too. It pays for energy bills to keep us warm and illuminated with light. It allows us to cook food too, and keep it cold and fresh so it lasts longer and doesn't go off.

So money can be used wisely as an energy to enhance our wellbeing, even if it doesn't guarantee it.

No matter how much money we throw at our health though, people still seem to get ill. Of course, our lifestyle might cause us to have an accident. We could crash our Ferrari or break a leg or arm on a skiing holiday. Smoking those expensive cigars and imbibing just a little too much whisky, wine, or beer might take its toll on our lungs or our livers.

There are, however, centenarians who've smoked like chimneys all their lives. It's debated whether low rates of heart disease in the butter and wine loving French is an urban myth, bad science, or massaging of statistics. For every report on how overindulgence causes disease, there will always be notable exceptions to the rule.

THE TICKING TIME BOMB

Wellbeing and mindfulness seem to be hot topics in the media at the time of writing this book. A simple Internet search will yield no end of articles on how meditation reduces symptoms of PTSD, or how yoga helps with weight loss, or even delaying the onset of dementia.

The healthcare industry is also facing a ticking time bomb of how it will deal with the onslaught of an increasing population that is living longer.

Right now, in the UK, ten-million people are over sixty-five years old. The latest projections are that the number will have nearly doubled to around nineteen-million by 2050. Within this total, the number of very old people grows even faster. The same shifting demographic exists in most modern countries.

So, in the Western World at least, Big Thinking is required on lifestyle choices. Undoubtedly, changes in the education system might help us get started at an early age. I hope that whatever is learned, trickles into the so-called Third World in time. In passing, I have always wondered where the Second World is.

There have been some good initiatives for several decades already. Last century we saw health warnings on packets of cigarettes, and now smoking is banned indoors in public spaces. School meals are being tinkered with to reduce the amount of fried food.

We're told to take our Five a Day. Alcoholic drinks are being labelled with their calorie content. These are all examples of good initiatives and, I am sure, the precursors of many more to come.

We spend trillions annually making people better after they have become ill. In 2009, around 70% of Americans were prescribed at least one drug, and half were given two or more. Conspiracists will argue that this state of affairs has been brought about by the conniving of the pharmaceutical industry. We should remember that the bright scientists creating these drugs are human too and probably take some of their own pills. While there may be a few Fat Cats creaming off the profits, most of the people designing drugs do it because they care.

At this stage in our evolution, dedicated healthcare professionals are just using all their experience and knowledge to help people who have succumbed to illnesses. Some amazing strides forward are being made with smart cancer drugs. The increasing longevity of recipients of donated organs is a testament to the cunning and skill of surgical teams. Nanotechnology and 3D printers are being used to replace parts of humans that have worn out. We even have a local vet who builds new limbs for dogs and cats.

Just imagine, though, if the solution to the problem of a crumbling health service, which itself is ill at a macroscopic level, lies in the microcosm of each of us.

If every individual took responsibility for their own wellbeing, an enormous burden would be removed from society as a whole. I am not referring to everyone paying for their own healthcare.

By taking ownership for our individual wellbeing, we can scale up and embrace the wellbeing of all humanity. Then, as sentient life-forms, we can begin to think collectively about the wellbeing of all life and the planet herself. We truly become custodians and guardians of the planet as opposed to simply being users.

THE BODY TEMPLE

We live in a very special place in the cosmos. We know it's currently the only planet in our Solar System that our bodies could survive without a spacesuit and life support system. Indeed, you can see Spaceship Earth as our life support system. Go just seven miles up to where jet planes cruise and you will die in seconds.

As we cruise around the Sun at 67,000 miles an hour, we're fortunately for the most part stuck to our home planet by the force of love – which some call gravity, of course. As we walk around, safely bonded to the planet's surface, the innards of our individual life support system are carried around by our skeleto-muscular framework. It is all held from leaking out into the world by our fascias, to varying degrees of success.

Somewhere on top of this thing we call a human, is a brain and some sensors we call eyes, ears, noses, and a tongue with which we assess the world around us.

The massive organ that is our skin, acts as our contacting interface with the world, and our comfort blanket too.

The fact we are able to even do this is nothing short of miraculous. Although, our physical form is just the smallest tip of the iceberg that is Us.

The temple of our body can be seen as a three-sided structure. Sometimes it's referred to as The Triad of Health, and drawn as an equilateral triangle. At the base, we have 'Structure'. The two sides are conventionally labelled as 'Chemical' and 'Mental'. There are several variations to this model.

Our traditional healthcare service has become quite masterful at repairing broken structures, and rebalancing chemistries with counteracting drugs. Very little attention is paid to the mental aspect of our wellbeing. If it is treated, the condition itself is often seen in isolation and labelled as such and such a syndrome or disorder.

What is not generally recognised is that the seed of virtually all dis-ease has a mind-based component and that applies to some accidents too.

This, of course, is nothing new. Eastern medicine looks at the mind, body, and spirit. All that has happened with Western medicine is that as it's become rather good at the techie stuff, it has forgotten some of the basics. This presents us with an amazing opportunity.

We don't have to throw the baby out with the bath water and say, "East is best and West is a pest." We can pick and choose the best bits from both schools of thought and learning, and come up with a 1+1=3 scenario.

IT'S THE THOUGHT THAT COUNTS

The essential difference between the philosophies of the East and West is the source of the illness and the ownership of solution. It's all too common and easy to blame our doctors if we don't get well and the government if we get ill.

In Eastern medicine, the illness is seen as a symptom of a wider malaise and underlying cause. The responsibility to get well lies with the patient. The medical professional is there to assist and point them back on track. To be fair to Western medicine, many practitioners are waking up to this way of thinking.

There have been loads of studies on the placebo effect where someone is given, for example, a sugar pill and their symptoms seem to lessen. Just the thought we might get better seems to have equal, if not greater, effect than a drug that might make us better.

What is not yet understood and appreciated is how much our thoughts cause imbalances in our chemical systems, which leads to deterioration in our structure. To fully appreciate where dis-ease comes from and how it affects us, we again have to attribute different thought forms to where they come from in our body.

Dis-eases of the gut and heart are the most readily understood. If we are worried about the future or the past, or perhaps harbour guilt, the related thought forms emanate from our gut mind. The resulting symptoms are irritation of the bowel and digestive disorders. If people are unlucky in love and carry low self-esteem (low self-love), this weakens the heart and leads to circulatory conditions.

Fears are known to weaken our kidney function. More subtly, if we are prevented from speaking our truth, it can affect our lungs and make us prone to sore throats.

The thought forms that lead to mindfalls are perhaps the most insidious. As they run around and around in our brain, they weaken the neurons, and can lead to dementia and strokes.

SPIRITS ON A HUMAN JOURNEY

The physical body mapped on to the Triad of Health only tells part of the story of who and what we are. While it is a valuable and useful model, our physical body is only the tip of the iceberg of our being.

Around all living things is an auric field, which stretches out for some metres from the physical form. It also connects us with the collective consciousness across all space and time, so in some ways it can be thought of as being infinite. I can teach people to feel it within a few minutes and see it within a few weeks.

If someone has a dis-ease in their physical body, with a little training and some attunement, it is possible to see disruptions and discolourations in the aura.

When you learn to perceive the aura, you could be forgiven for thinking that it's generated by the body. When attending those who shed their mortal coil, attuned people report seeing the aura leave.

A more interesting way to see the aura is that it distills our body from itself into physical space. The body is a crystallisation of a higher dimensional aura into the Physical Plane. When people talk about us not being humans on a spiritual journey but spirits on a human journey, this is how that works.

So, while we are examples of incarnate spirit, as by the way is every plant, insect, fish, and animal, there are plenty of discarnate spirits floating around too. By this, I am not referring to dear departed humans and your Aunt Maud, but kind of the flotsam and jetsam of the spirit world. They are all looking for homes.

If the Triad of our Health is out of skew, this causes a weakness in the auric field and undesirable entities can latch on. Most of them are not malevolent but more like lost and confused. They manifest in the form of rashes and allergies and are often intolerant to foodstuffs. As such, when we have them on board, our resistance is lowered to things that make us ill.

There is nothing to be alarmed or frightened about here. Incredible as it seems, our bodies comprise of 90% parasites and bacteria, and only 10% is what you might think of as human.

Discarnate spirits latch on and off us all the time. If you have ever had an unexplained feeling of dread or depression, you will have experienced this phenomenon.

Now, if you think I have gone a bit weird on you, it's about to get weirder. Our auras carry an imprint of all our predecessors. This gets encoded in our DNA, and may be the bulk and function of the 'dark matter' in DNA that has geneticists so puzzled.

The implication of this to our wellbeing is that we are predisposed to the dis-eases and intolerances of our ancestors.

So, if we harbour an illness, not only do we put a strain on our healthcare system and loved ones, but we have an obligation to our ancestors too. This gives an additional incentive and opportunity when we enhance our wellbeing.

BREADCRUMB: *To understand how the aura and the Triad of Health integrate and interact with each other, find out how to make an equilateral triangle into a 3D object. When you've done that, create a copy of it and turn it on its head. Then contra-rotate the two objects you've created.*

A WELLER BEING

When we begin to comprehend how dis-ease has a spiritual component, it leads us to new possibilities for ways of being. When we learn to meditate, what happens as a by-product is that our aura changes colour and vibrates at higher frequencies.

In passing, I should point two things out. Firstly, I did not plan to write a book banging on and on about meditation, it just keeps popping up. Secondly, when people talk about auras, colours, frequency, and vibrations, these terms are only analogous to their electromagnetic counterparts in the Physical Plane. Another way to see raised vibration is that we start to resonate with higher levels of consciousness and awareness. I digress.

The raising of our vibration makes it harder for the less desirable discarnate entities to latch on. This in turn makes us less prone to illness. This gives us access to a whole new set of tools with which to heal. What's more, any healing we perform at an auric level passes up and down the timelines. Bizarre as it sounds, we can heal the past and the future whilst also sorting things out in the present.

MY BAROMETER

It might seem strange at first but we can use the concepts of money, time, thought, and love as barometers to assess our wellbeing. They also act as a measure how successfully we are weaving magic into our lives.

Take money, for example. What's not important with money is how much of it you have stacked up – it's more about flow and what you do with it. Too much money just stuck in a bank can lead to stagnation in our aura.

The perfect amount of money is to be bringing in something like 5-10% more than you need at any one time. Another measure of how 'well' you are doing, is that the money you need pops along before you need it in time. Any surplus can be wisely deployed to enhance our wellbeing with treats like holidays, meals out, and charitable donations, if that's your bag.

In the same way, if we always have enough time for both our own activities and the support of others, it signifies we have everything in balance.

Our thoughts also indicate how well we are being. For starters, not having to worry about money or missing a deadline stops many negative thought forms in their tracks. Note, of course, if we have too much money, we might start having fearful thoughts that we don't have enough or that it might run out.

Many people now are fearful, for example, of how money will provide for them in a potentially elongated retirement. Strangely, thought forms associated with such fears can even seed dementia.

The other barometer is how much we love life in general, ourselves, what we are doing, and what our loved ones are doing.

Looking back on my life, I've been pretty lucky in all these areas. Remember that I came from a poor family and everything that has come my way is through my own endeavour. Of course, there have been times when cash has been tight. There was a period of a few years after I graduated from university when love was sadly lacking.

Before I discovered meditation, I was in an angry, throwing-toys-out-of-the-pram place, with the people I was in business with. Thoughts of revenge and self-righteousness raged around my cranium. Time, fortunately, has always been on my side and I have always felt I could get things done and that everything I desired would come to be 'all in Good Time'.

At the time of writing, if I mentally scan my body and my world for my general wellbeing, all is pretty good apart from one thing. I have not even thought about this until writing these very words. The flow of cash into my business is a bit sticky and haphazard. If it flowed in more quantity and regularity, I could get more done and potentially help more people.

My reaction to this is not to panic but to direct attention to it. Historically, the last 12 months needed me to direct attention to supporting elderly relatives. So the situation is merely a symptom, and not a fundamental malaise. It can and will resolve itself, especially now it's percolated into my consciousness.

THE CATCH

The ideal, of course, is that these four measures in our lives - of money, time, wellbeing and love - are all in the positive. If money is tight but you are loved and have some time to generate some more cash, you can ride a storm. The measure of which we should be the most mindful is the nature and content of our thoughts.

One of the potential pitfalls we can become unstuck by is that the more our magical powers grow and develop, the more any negative thought forms are able to manifest. So, if you are going to have thoughts, you have to make them Good Ones. It is easy to see how we can easily go into a downwards spiral if the wheels fall off the bus.

By seeing lack of money, time, and love as symptoms, not conditions, we are able to address the root condition.

It is after all the thought that counts.

HOW ARE YOU DOING?

If the wheels have fallen off our bus, or are just a bit wobbly, a pit stop is what is required. For me, a walk in nature is one of the most useful ways to do this.

As you walk, leave all feelings of anger, remorse, regret, and self-loathing behind you, and see your current condition as symbolic of your journey so far. Just imagine you are walking into a brighter future.

On your walk, notice if the ground under your feet gets muddy or sloppy, and how you are thinking. Observe how your thoughts change as the path narrows and widens. If you are fortunate enough to be able to take in a view, stop. Then see how your world looks.

Notice too how your thoughts alter as you look down and up.

Let one idea to help you change your world pop in. When you get back to base, take action. Then sleep on it and observe how the universal flow attracts just what you need to help you, towards you over the coming days.

| path |

KARMA IS A POWERFUL CONCEPT THAT ALLOWS US TO GAIN PERSPECTIVE ON BOTH WHY WE ARE HERE AND WHAT DIRECTION WE SHOULD TAKE IN LIFE. THE TERM 'KARMA' IS ALSO ONE THAT CAN EASILY GET HIJACKED AND MISUSED.

Karma is not some kind of cosmic retribution system. It is not a ledger of all the good and bad things you have done. This model for karma is one that only surfaces when people want to exercise a degree of control over others. Simply put, karma is your collective experience and learnings to date. If you want to think of it as being accrued over multiple lifetimes, that's completely optional.

It is also thought that our karmic path, or mission, can be preordained and pre-agreed by ourselves. Again, it is somewhat academic if this is true or not, but just thinking that it might be can have real-world benefits. When you flip from thinking that the world might be against you, to seeing all events as opportunities for learning and growth, a kinder world presents itself.

The metaphysical stance is that karma goes with the soul from lifetime to lifetime. One theory I heard was that the parts of soul can incarnate in many bodies both simultaneously and backwards and forwards in space and time. Also, each incarnate being can contain multiple 'soul parts'. This means any cosmic ledger recording our good or bad deeds would be tricky to maintain.

A materialistic explanation for all of this could be that learning is carried, and passed on, by our DNA and RNA from generation to generation. I am half my mother and father and, in turn, a quarter of my four grandparents. This could explain how learnings are carried forward in time.

Karma, though, does not just work linearly forwards with Time's Arrow. A shaman taught me a trick some years ago of how to send messages, or learnings, back in time to earlier versions of you.

Karma describes a path of learning and advancement, and that is the context in which it is used when we want to awaken our inner magician. Karma is simply the sum of all our past learnings combined with our intent in the now and our actions going forward. If you so choose, this can include past and future incarnations too, but this is somewhat academic as there is only one thing you can change and that's what you are thinking and doing right now!

In the context of karma, there are only two types of events – ones that confirm we are on-path and ones that tell us we have strayed off it. When we are on it, life is a breeze. When we fall off the path, life is a struggle.

YOUR KARMIC PATH

Without any degree of conscious awareness, each of us has been acting out our own pre-agreed karmic path already. Everything we have done in our life so far is perfect. It is perfect insofar as you are reading this and, irrespective of your state of health, you are living and breathing.

What is even better still is that the very fact you are on the path to 'void karma' means that you are keen to make improvements in your life – even if your life is OK at the moment. For example, it's a great idea to go for massage and 'therapy' even when you don't have a 'dis-ease'.

If you disagree with this stance and think that things aren't so perfect, this is also good news. Many people think that whatever life they are living is cast in stone, or dictated by external agencies, such that they have given up and in this way subjugated themselves.

You will hear it said that nobody can breathe for you, eat for you, or love for you. In the same way, nobody can show or tell you the path to enlightenment.

If anybody tells you that they have found 'The Secret to Life, The Universe, and Everything', don't believe them. We each have to find our own path.

All systems, including the voiding of karma tool I am about to share, are just tools and signposts. While I have done my best to make my approach as baggage-free as possible, it is only one view of how things work. It definitely is not The Answer, but hopefully contains some clues as to where some of the answers lie.

In the same way, nobody can or should tell you how to live your life. Your life is your gift to do with as you wish.

What is both ethical to dispense and wise to use, is a map by which you can better find your own way. Like all maps, they are both liable to change and benefit from being updated by people who have followed them, noticed new waypoints and routes, and corrected any errata.

It should also be noted that a particular map does not have to be the same for everyone. There as many maps as there are people on the planet – past, present, and future.

The maps, however, do have similarities, and certain end destinations are shared in common.

So, I am sure I will grab your attention if I tell you that it is entirely possible to live a happy, magical, exciting, and fulfilled life. Also, that this can be done whilst gaining a degree of enlightenment along the way – and in harmony and ecology with nature and your fellow women and men.

The key to mapping out this particular type of future lies in looking at where we have come from already and taking stock.

Once this is done, we can then map out a whole new course.

VOIDING KARMA

The word 'void' has many meanings and semantics, as it can be used as an adjective, a verb, and a noun. Examples of its definition that apply in the context we are using it here are:

Adjective:
- useless; ineffectual; vain
- without contents; empty

Verb:
- to empty; discharge; evacuate
- to make ineffectual

Noun:
- an empty space; emptiness
- a gap or opening

So when we void karma, we empty and 'zero' what is there now by evacuating what is already there and we make a gap and an opening for new stuff to come in. So how does this work?

Linguistically, often when an 'a' is put in front of a word, we don't negate it but we neutralise it.

Examples would be 'sexual' and 'asexual' and 'gnostic' and 'agnostic'. They are respectively different from pseudo-words like 'unsexual' and 'ungnostic'.

The addition of the 'a' does not mean the opposite of, but, more subtly, the absence of. Accordingly, the majority of people spend their lives 'a-voiding' facing up to their karmic purpose.

So when we 'avoid' something we are not so much 'not voiding' it, but somewhat skirting around the edges of it.

Now, there is nothing wrong with this at all. Incarnating and experiencing the Earth experience is a good thing in itself. If you 'a-void' karma, it is thought that you just come back time and time again anyway.

So what's the benefit to voiding if it doesn't matter anyway?

Well, for some the earthly existence is not so joy-full, for some it's dull, and for others, there is a suspicion that there are untold riches to be had if only they knew how. It is to those that are latterly motivated, I should stress that the riches on offer are not just financial.

Voiding of karma is something so subtle that it is also quite elusive. It is more an intent than an action in itself and once you make the decision to void your karma, the karmic purpose itself doesn't so much disappear but it crystallises and appears in full view.

We understand what it is we came here to do.

At the same time, something incredibly magical happens, 'the universe' acknowledges that we have realised what it's all about and it sits up, takes notice, and starts delivering 'stuff' to you on a plate. 'The universe', by the way, is anything you want it to be – God, god, the Source, or the Collective Consciousness – or just Lady Luck.

I am a-gnostic about it and feel it doesn't require 'knowing' or 'not-knowing'. It just is. In my book, real-world, tangible results alone are the proof of the pudding.

In essence, life takes on a magical quality, you become incredibly lucky, and all around you sit up and take notice and want some of it. You know you have arrived.

CLEARING THE DECKS

All of this is, of course, easier to say than it is to do. Just when we think we get things under control, that curved ball can get thrown our way. Dealing with such unexpected pitfalls is the key here.

When we look at life's events from a karmic perspective, there is no such thing as a bad happening. If something good happens, our response should be to say, "Thank You." If something not so good happens, we should also say, "Thank You." We thank it for the lesson and the learning.

We can also apply this thinking retrospectively, back in time. Think back to all those tough times. You are still alive and you have experience. Thank them right now, and something magical will start to happen. Either those types of events never appear in our lives or, if they do, they don't affect us in the same way.

THE WAY OF THE WIZARD

When adversity and serendipity are welcomed equally with open arms, we can never fall off our path.

So, as you may have surmised by now, my path has been a relatively easy one, comparatively. To reiterate, the aim of this book is not to brag but merely to share that an alternative way is not so hellish.

When I was a boy, I dreamt of being a train driver or an astronaut. I still want to be the latter. As a teenager, I tuned into a career in science. A university degree in electrickery manifested with ease. While at university, I specialised in TV technology, and getting a dream job in the broadcast industry became my goal. As I mentioned, both the BBC and ITV offered me a job. I chose 'Aunty Beeb' solely because the money was slightly better, as the job was shift based and paid great overtime.

Until my mid-forties, my career path was driven by both earning money and professional pride. In parallel, I had a burning curiosity to learn how technology worked and how it could be used and enhanced. I was being paid for playing with high technology. I was so on path, surely?

The idea of being an author, a specialist in writer's unblocking, and now being called by others a wizard, alchemist, oracle, and mystic was certainly not on the cards.

These are all labels I resisted at first, but now use sparingly with audiences who are open to their real significance. I read the Way of the Wizard by Deepak Chopra, and then realised I must have turned into one. Incidentally, one client even calls me Dumbledore, but – by way of balance – my soul mate refers to me as Dobby the House Elf, at the weekends.

This type of path and what monikers are ascribed with, I have discovered, is not something we can choose for ourselves. Any magic that is dispensed does not come from us but through us.

This path does, however, feel like the one I incarnated for. Being adept at broadcast and Internet technologies really helps when it comes to getting messages out there, so my early life is by no means a waste.

If there has been one trait that links my two disparate careers, it is this. I love finding out how things work and then innovating ways we can make them work even better still.

So when I discovered weird things starting to happen when I meditated, my curiosity was piqued and I felt compelled to look into it all further. At the time, the scientific community seemed to be blinkered and sceptic about all things slightly woo-woo, so I looked for the wisdom of ages in esoteric writings. I used to be angry at such entrenchment, but now I realise everyone is free to choose their path.

All are called but by no means all are ready. In any event, the separation from Source has resulted in humankind being masters of the Physical Plane. This is a Good Thing and part of the overall plan. Humans, by the way, aren't a million or so years old, they have been around since the dawn of time but not in a form we might recognise.

I have now been studying with two esoteric schools for the best part of ten years, and some of what I have learned cannot be shared openly. The initiate must find their own path. The clues of who I worked with are at the back of this book, but there are many paths of return. I encourage you to allow yours be shown to you.

I do find traditional mystery teachings far more complicated than they need to be. Accordingly, my strategy is to disseminate what is essentially the same information, but in a simpler and more accessible way. That is my hope at least. My books are like Trojan Horses, as the inside contains more magic than the cover might suggest. I hasten to add that the insides are not a marauding bunch of soldiers but a set of keys to open the reader's heart and mind.

As there is no way I could possibly be where I am now by planning, I allow the universe to dictate my direction. I trust higher powers to show me the way. I had no idea we, as humans, can do what I find I can do now.

Healing a budgie over Skype, levitating (by accident), and seeing past and future lives in the aura are just some of the stranger things I find myself doing.

What I can only surmise is that there must be more magic to be unleashed still, and that there are probably an infinite set of rungs for us all to climb.

When on this pathless path, if I do make an error of judgement, adversity will soon show me that I have either gone the wrong way or I have something yet to learn. For the most part, I just live a timeful, mindful, joyful, and playful existence.

BREADCRUMB: the next time something upsets you, meditate on why you are upset and where the upset resides. Then ask the 'upset' what its real purpose is.

THE CATCH

There is no catch if we learn from resistance and confirm we are on path from the endless stream of opportunity. Where we might come unstuck, though, is when we are given multiple choices and don't know which path to take.

When we begin on our magical journey, we can manifest so many opportunities that we don't know which way to turn. Such multiple opportunity can lead to confusion.

We can end up juggling too many balls and dropping a few. Letting them drop gracefully is not failure but a way to get back on path.

AWAKENING YOUR ORACLE

As mentioned, there are so many routes to enlightenment. There are so many teachers, both alive and dead, who can help us on our way. There are false prophets too, but they all play a role. Some of them are not aware of their level of awakening, in the same way a fish doesn't know it is wet.

So how do you choose?

Which path is right for you?

The easy way to find out is to seek guidance. We are fortunate to have two guidance systems. One is internal and the other discarnate.

When we have a choice to make, we can check in with our internal guidance system. We can ask our gut-mind for a Yes or a No. If we get a No, just then ask what would have to change to make it a Yes. If you get a straight Yes, go for it. If you get a definite No, avoid it. If it's a Maybe, wait for the conditions and timing to change and for it to turn into a Yes.

Externally, we all have discarnate guides we can tune into. They have many names. Some call them Angels, others Ascended Masters. In the next chapter, I will share a mechanism with you by which they operate and who these 'guides' are.

Whether they are imaginary or real is academic so long as imagining that they are real helps. They communicate with us in various ways. Some clairaudient people can actually tune into their voice. The clairvoyant receive images, and very often in dreams, too. The claircogniscent get their messages in the form of 'knowings' that they couldn't possibly know.

For example, in a book I wrote, I wanted Mars and the Earth to be on opposite sides of the Sun on a certain date over a century from now. I chose a date 'at random' and later found an online Solar System that I could wind forward. For the date I had chosen arbitrarily to fit in with the plot, the two planets were exactly where I wanted them to be.

We can also ask for guidance in the form of signs, signposts, and metaphors. The tip I mentioned earlier, where we go for a walk and watch for a sign, being a great example.

Often, if we ignore the first sign, we might be reminded. If three people tell you to read a book, you should read it.

At all times, be mindful of how easy or difficult your life is. This is the biggest signifier of whether you are off your path or on it. Once you find your way, the most important quality to be embraced is that of trust.

It's a bit like learning to swim. At first we have water-wings to help us let go of the side. Next, we swim breadth-wise in the shallow end so we can put our feet down if we need to. The next step is to take the water-wings off and swim lengths into the deep end. While it is scary, it's also exciting.

| aha |

IT MIGHT SEEM REMARKABLE BUT, IN ALL PROBABILITY, THOMAS ALVA EDISON DID NOT ACTUALLY HAVE A LIGHT-BULB MOMENT WHEN HE DIDN'T INVENT THE LIGHT-BULB.

For starters, what he came up with was the longer lasting filament and a bulb that could easily be replaced. The Edison Screw is still used in some bulbs today, but the filament technology has evolved considerably. The electric light-bulb itself was more of an on-going development than a flash of inspiration.

Apparently, Edison tried around ten-thousand different materials before he found an exotic type of bamboo which gave out light for forty hours when a current was passed through it. At the time, this was amazing and he was spurned on by his vision of only wanting candles to be afforded by the rich. He didn't invent the light-bulb though, as he only discovered a longer lasting filament.

Edison was a visionary and very, very inventive, but he was primarily an empiricist. He may have used a cumbersome version of the scientific method but he kept copious notes and often found a use for one failed material he had tested in another application down the line. He was both a master of the spin off and also one of the progenitors of venture capitalism. He was expert at getting money from financiers and putting on a show.

If he'd had a light-bulb moment, however, he would have come up with a vision for the perfect filament type in less than a split second. We should also bear in mind that people have been having light-bulb moments for thousands of years before the actual emergence of the light-bulb.

Archimedes had a 'eureka moment' in his bath when he worked out how to use the displacement of water to assay the quality of a gold crown. St Paul had a blinding flash of divine realisation on the road to Damascus. Isaac Newton experienced his 'aha moment' when he got the whole of the theory of gravity in less than a second. It's said that it took him the whole of the rest of his life to work out the mathematics.

Irrespective of what we call them, they happen in less than a second and seem to run against our thought stream, coming from no-where. They are not so much an Ethereal Whisper as they are an Ethereal Shout. When I wrote my book on the subject, I found very little research had been carried out as to their nature. I couldn't readily find any real reference as to when the phrase 'light-bulb moment' entered common usage.

As I wrote the book, I found I had to channel information as to their true source and nature. I divined that they were thought forms that came from the collective consciousness. I also found out they were not just whole brain events where the left and right brain wire and fire together in synchronism.

When we experience an aha moment, we experience a Whole Mind Event. For an instant, we are connected to The All – the one Source. We literally 'see the light'. The inspirational thought form enters our physical form, either at our crown or at the back of our skull. This is why we say that we had this idea 'off the top of our head', or that 'something is at the back of my mind'. Our language always gives away what is really going on.

Once the thought form enters, it gets routed to our base chakra, which checks in with Mother Earth that it is safe and ecological for both us and the planet. It then pops in on our sacral mind to ensure it meets our needs. Our solar plexus, and gut mind, gives it a green light. Our heart mind falls in love with it. It then pops into our right brain which 'sees' the whole vision before our left brain fills in the detail.

If you are like Archimedes, you might even engage your throat mind and shout, "Eureka."

FUTURE MEMORIES

The exact location of our memory is still proving elusive. This is because it sits in the collective thought field. As we flow through our three dimensions of space with a forward arrow of time, we are prewired to be able to tap into past memories. Our DNA acts as a tuning fork, so that the memories we can tap into most readily are our own.

As all thought is stored in the collective, we can also tap into future memories. Again, the ones we are most tuned into are those that comprise the thoughts and experiences we are yet to have. To do this, just two things are needed: One, a little practice, and two, to suspend our disbelief and imagine that it might be true.

If this sounds a bit bizarre, we already possess neurology that works ahead of time. Neurologists have discovered that our gut-mind operates a few seconds ahead of our conscious awareness. This phenomenon gives rise to the super-sensibility of Near-field Precognition. The field in question being the 'time field' we walk down. It is our gut-mind that 'knows' who is at the other end of the phone slightly before it rings. It also stops us pulling out at T-junctions and stepping off the pavement because it 'sees' oncoming danger before we are aware of it consciously.

How often have you said, "Phew, that was close, that car/bike/lorry/bus came out of nowhere!"?

PRE-SCIENCE

Adding a hyphen to a word often gives us insight, or in-sight, into its true meaning. Prescience means to see something ahead of time. When we hyphenate it to pre-science, it gives us a clue as to how future scientific knowledge can leak back in time. Now, I know this statement is everything but scientific in its nature, but such a mechanism might be how Da Vinci came to draw helicopters several hundred years before they first flew.

Clearly some more research is needed before the scientific community will validate such phenomena, but my personal belief is that such investigations would be of great value. Sages and mystics just work with such super-abilities daily and don't worry too much about how they work. Their intuition, or inner-tuition, just tells them to trust what information comes their way when they tap into the collective.

These days, we call these illuminations light-bulb moments, but they are really 'moments of light'. They are a natural phenomenon, which are only dampened by disbelief in them.

I know of many people who have experienced such moments in the shower or even while peeing. One of the reasons for this is that water is the conductor of the universal 'mind-stuff'.

Such 'future memories' seem to come our way when we are 'not-thinking', that is: when we are in the meditative state. Our future self knows what we will know and discover hours, days, and years from now. Authors can tap into the words we have yet to write and musicians into the songs they have to sing.

In the dream state, our conscious mind is quiescent but, often, the dreams speak to us in allegory or metaphor. August Kekulé, the Belgian chemist, was working on the structure of the benzene molecule but could not work out how the six carbon and six hydrogen atoms could be connected. When he dreamt of a snake biting its tail, he awoke with the concept of the benzene ring. He had unwittingly uncovered the basis for modern organic chemistry.

Incidentally, when such ideas and illuminations come our way, if we ignore them, we often get reminded about them. If, after two or three attempts, we don't take up on an idea, it pops back into the collective for someone else to capitalise upon it.

This is why we might have an idea, do nothing with it, and then find someone else makes something of it a few years down the line.

So, if our future self is sending us a message, we would be foolish to ignore it.

BREADCRUMB: *Just imagine right now that you have a message for a younger version of you. Send it to yourself in the past right now. Next, ask yourself who gave the present you the message to send the past you a message. Extrapolate.*

LEAVING CUBELAND

If we imagine a two-dimensional flatland with no Up, as a higher three-dimensional being we can see how entrapped its occupants might be. If a flat being met another head on, she or he would have to go sideways and along a bit, and then sideways again, to get around the other. With the gift of our three dimensional vision, we could see that one could just leap over the other easily, if only they had an Up.

If a five-dimensional being looks down on us, they would find it amusing that for us to get from a point in the past to one in the future, we have to pass through every intervening second, minute, and hour to get there. Everything takes time. This is not a bad thing intrinsically, as it gives us the ability to experience our lives.

Aspects of our being are multidimensional in nature. The Minor Arcana of the Tarot describes us as nine-dimensional beings having a three-dimensional experience.

There are four planes of being that we tap into all the time. They are each occupied by discarnate intelligences and awarenesses that we can connect with.

We occupy and experience the Physical Plane. This is the reality we experience in our waking hours.

The Physical Plane is connected to the fifth-dimensional Formative Plane by the dimension of time. The Formative Plane is the plane of processes, or connections.

The Formative Plane connects to the seventh-dimensional Creative Plane through the dimension of light. The Creative Plane contains all potential just waiting to percolate down to be enabled by a process.

The Creative Plane connects to the ninth-dimensional Archetypal Plane through the dimension of thought. The Archetypal Plane contains all seed ideas and concepts.

When we experience an aha moment, what happens is that, for an instant, we connect with all these planes at the same time. In a flash, we get the seed idea from the Archetypal Plane. We see all the potential applications it can deliver in the Creative Plane. We get a glimpse of how to implement it 'in time' from the Formative Plane. We 'see' how that idea might make us richer than our wildest dreams while we live out our lives in the Physical Plane.

THE ABOVE TO THE BELOW

The multi-dimensional model of ourselves gives us an understanding of our place in the scheme of things. We agree to incarnate as a spirit into the Earth Plane. In doing this we became a connector of the Above to the Below. We came from Source so we could look back at ourselves.

By agreeing to forget where we came from and why, we are left to wander on the Earth Plane and to wonder. By doing this, we get to discover new ways to experience a physical existence.

Humans have been around much longer than is generally accepted, although we have only adopted our current humanoid form for around two-million-or-so years. We have evolved incredibly, and around a million years or so ago, developed this amazing ability of being self-aware. This evolution is still going on and we have much more to discover about why we are here and what is possible while we are here.

Future versions of us do have this knowledge and we have a nascent capability to tune into who we might be. This, of course, sets up a causal loop that entangles the Present Us with what we are to evolve into in the future.

What this means is that tuning into aha moments is not just about coming up with bright ideas. When we experience our aha, we also tune into our future karmic path.

HOW I TUNED IN

My first memory of experiencing an aha moment out of the blue was in a maths class. The teacher was struggling to get the basics of algebra across to a bunch of twelve year olds. I'd picked up what he was trying to teach ages ago, so was looking out of the window in a dreamy state, wishing he'd get on with things. He must have spotted me, and said, "Evans, boy, do you get it?"

I replied that I did, so he held up his piece of chalk and asked me to come up and explain it. Although quite bright, I was incredibly nervous about standing up in front of the class, much less at explaining algebra. Somewhere between leaving my desk and walking towards the blackboard, I had a vision. I drew a see-saw and put the algebraic terms on each side of it. As I moved things around, I showed how the see-saw could be made to balance and the equation be solved. To this day, I don't think this kind of visual mathematics is taught in schools. More's the pity, as the whole class got it and the teacher was off the hook.

Later on in my career as a broadcast engineer, cameramen (as they were mostly men in those days) would approach me with a problem. Within a split second, knowing the cameras backwards and having an appreciation of elecktrickery, I'd come up with a solution.

It was in my late-forties when I had the light-bulb moment that it would be a great idea to write a book about light-bulb moments. Being a practical chap, the book is in two parts. The first half of The Art and Science of Light Bulb Moments explains how to have them on demand, as opposed to waiting for them to come along. The second half explains how to make sure the best ideas actually happen and don't get away.

During the middle of writing it, I got stuck writing chapter nine. I use a technique with writers who are blocked using free association with words and images on a Mind Map. So I used the words 'light', 'bulb', and 'moment' as my seeds and a veritable cascade ensued.

I saw that our thoughts come in flavours, and each type of thought form comes from different dimensional layers. I had been studying the Tarot for a few years and I saw that the Major and Minor Arcana described this in detail, but had obscured the detail in layers of imagery. I saw then that my mission was to demystify the mystery of how we got here and what our purpose was. The secret was buried in the cards.

Being an engineer, not only did I set about explaining what the cards really said in layperson's language, I also invented a few ways they could be used in practice. The Major Arcana, or Flavours of Thought, could be used to create spells, or Recipes for Fresh Thinking. The Minor Arcana, or Planes of Being, could be used in an oracular fashion to tune into our future self.

This means we can all become seers, or see-ers. With such ability, we can tune into the most perfect future world, from all possible futures, and entangle with it. This will allow us to bring Heaven even more down to Earth.

In the two books that followed, called This We Know, and This We Are, I wrote two postscripts describing a possible future for humanity in one-hundred and two-hundred years time. This vision arrived in less than a second. It will just take us a little linear time to get there.

THE CATCH

When I first learned I could experience aha moments on demand, my fear was that I would be awash with ideas.

I was already a creative guy, so getting even more ideas might tip me into overload. To compound this, with permission from a client, I discovered I could tune into their future self too. With more than enough thoughts of my own, the last thing I needed was those of other people to think about too.

As it transpired, my fears were groundless. After a short time, I found that the quantity of thoughts diminished but the quality went up. If a stray thought form from, or for, a client turned up, I learned to recognise it as not being for me. When such gems appear, I freely give them away, which means they don't clog up my mental sphere and I am free to channel my own stuff.

TUNING IN

It will come as no surprise, as it features in most chapters, that the best way by far to tune into aha moments is through meditation. I also find walking meditation works a treat too.

One of the reasons it works so well is that, when we walk, the opposite motion of our arms and legs stirs up the universal mind-stuff and causes the two sides of our brain to synchronise.

There is, however, a simpler way to generate an aha, and that's to ask. Just ask for some help with what you are working on and you will get an answer. Sometimes the answer comes back in literal form or a very clear inspiration.

Most often it comes by way of a sign. Occasionally, it will arrive in metaphorical form by way of a dream. All you have to do is be wide open to receive.

If it helps, you can also ask your future self for a sign or an enlightenment by way of an ethereal whisper.

The other technique which is worth practicing is to send messages back to your earlier self. Such messages are simple to send and hard for an unsuspecting earlier version of you to ignore. They are what make you who you are now.

To give you an idea of how this works, I am right now sending the idea of a see-saw as a way to solve algebraic formulae to that twelve-year-old version of me. I also genuinely only thought of that now, and the idea that I should send it came from a version of me a few seconds in the future.

I hope that notion hasn't tied you in too many temporal knots.

| healing |

IT IS INTERESTING THAT THE VERB 'TO HEAL' IS BOTH TRANSITIVE AND INTRANSITIVE.

What this means is that someone can heal us – heal [verb transitive]: to set right or repair.

Alternatively, we can heal ourselves – heal [verb intransitive]: to recover from an illness.

In both cases, it is worth noting that the best remedy by far is not to succumb to the illness that would require healing in the first place. In the UK alone, we collectively take over 100 million sick days off work a year. Just imagine the productivity improvements alone if this could be reduced. Introduction of wellbeing into our education system could be a good way to start.

If we are unfortunate enough to require externally applied healing, we take a pill, visit our doctor, and might possibly get referred to a specialist.

The malady will be identified and a remedy or course of treatment applied. Identifying the root cause is ideally undertaken as part of the diagnostic process, although sometimes this gets overlooked or ignored.

Conventional medicine will look to genetic predisposition, lifestyle, or accidental damage or trauma being the cause. In some cases, of course, this trauma may be mental. When a cause cannot be found, it is just put down to bad luck.

When healing is applied, the hope is that the condition will rectify itself and never reoccur. It is rare that the fundamental cause of any dis-ease is researched. This is partly because practitioners don't have the time, but also because illness is often seen in isolation as something that has to be cured and eliminated.

PAST TIMES PRESENT ISSUES

The double entendre in this subtitle is intentional.

When we see ourselves as beings with a past and future timeline that extends beyond our current lifetime, new opportunities for healing emerge, as do potential reasons for why we might get ill.

Remember that past life memories could occur either because our soul reincarnates or because our DNA contains a memory, or echo, of our ancestors.

Rupert Sheldrake championed the concept of morphic resonance. In it, he postulates that all life forms have a field around them that contains the imprint or information about its shape, form, and intricacies. It is this field that remembers how a salamander's tail is constructed so that it can regrow if it loses it. While we don't regrow limbs exactly, our body sheds cells continually and it is this field, or something like it, which helps us maintain our form from moment to moment. Note that the science around this is a bit shaky, so take this all metaphorically when it comes to healing and disease.

So, we resonate most strongly with the version of ourselves a second into the past and a second into the future. The morphic field 'remembers' who and what we are so that we don't vaporise or end up as a pile of atoms on the floor.

This same field resonates with all versions of us, and our predecessors in the past, and us and our descendants in the future. This means if there has been a dis-ease in our ancestry, we can be prone to fall ill to it. Conventional medicine will say it's in our genes.

There is a relatively new field of study called epigenetics.

It has been discovered that our DNA can, in fact, alter. Sometimes this can be spontaneous and, increasingly, geneticists are doing the tampering themselves. What is not quite accepted yet is that our thoughts can make the change too.

This means that, if we identify an illness and attribute a past life or genetic source to it, by disassociating from the seed notion that causes it, we can heal not only ourselves in the present but also our ancestors in the past. Bizarrely, the past is as malleable as the future.

TIME HEALS

I was attuned to channel Reiki energy in my early forties and used it mainly for healing myself, friends, family, and pets. As someone who wasn't born with healing ability per se, I now appreciate anyone can be attuned as a healer. When we attune to any healing energy, like Reiki, we become more vibrant and colours and sounds become brighter. We radiate in a new way and look younger. People ask if we have had treatment.

Undoubtedly, when I started to channel healing energy, my DNA changed in some subtle way as I picked up a different ability. Discovery of the genes linked to such alteration would be an amazing revelation. Not only would this lead to healthier people, but also to people who could make people healthier.

A few years later, when I studied past life regression and future life progression, I was introduced to an imaginative technique known as timeline therapy. Although I could see how it could be used, I felt intuitively that it was a bit clunky. Under light hypnosis, it takes a person back to just before a trauma occurred and refreshes the person in the present with the imprint of the previously healthy version of themselves. Bearing in mind that most dis-ease seeds in the mind, it does work, but essentially it was only a mental trick.

On the same past life regression course, I spontaneously saw through time. I perceived past and future lives in peoples' auras. I see this as actually seeing the morphic field around a person, which distills them into their current form. When I get into this mode, it is like time itself is 'softening'.

At first, I found this curious but felt it was a bit of a party trick so I kept it pretty quiet about it. I did find that I could also show past and future versions of myself to others too and teach pretty-much anyone how to do this. However, before long, I discovered a practical application of this strange phenomenon.

A friend of mine had a skiing accident and some ligament damage that resulted in a very swollen knee. I popped around just to apply some Reiki to help with general healing. As I did this, we 'softened' time between us and I asked her to look at her knee with me. Then I suggested she see the knee before the accident in the past, and after the healing had finished. In front of our eyes, the swelling went down. What was happening was that the knee pre-accident and post healing morphed into a less swollen knee.

She also had some surgery to reattach a ligament, but her overall recovery time, and discomfort, had been dramatically reduced. Her surgeon was really impressed at how quickly she healed. As belief is an intrinsic aspect of any healing, I am happy for him to take all the credit. For starters, he's done many more years of study than I have. I am a learner in this field. Also, collective belief aids when it comes to healing. If all concerned parties believe healing is taking place, it seems to work much faster and better.

Since then I have used this technique in a number of cases. Bear in mind, though, that I don't put myself out there as a healer, so only do this on a kind of 'as needs' basis. It seems to work equally well on physical trauma as it does with allergies and intolerances. Oddly enough, the only person I've not been able to help with it is me. I am still musing on why this might be the case. The answer may just lie in inner belief.

SOUL PARTS

Around the same time that I perceived past and future lives in the aura, I began to help people discard unwanted and undesirable habits and fears. I did this by assisting the trait leave the body as if it was a real entity or intelligence. In some early cases, I found that the undesirable tendencies returned, so I refined the technique. As the old tendency left, I helped the person replace it with a quality they wanted to bring into their lives. This seemed to do the trick and effected permanent and beneficial change.

I hadn't been on a course on how to do this. Clients who I could help just turned up, and it looked like the technique worked. As usual, I looked into what I had tripped over. It transpired I was performing a kind of exorcism, but without any trappings of religious dogma. Whatever entity leaves, makes all the choices itself, as we live on the planet of free will. I am continually surprised at what permutations this throws up.

I quickly learned that if I didn't fill the void left by the entity with a new essence, another discarnate force with a similar nature would quickly latch on.

What occurred to me was that we don't incarnate as one being but as an assemblage of soul parts. One goes to our head and acts as our consciousness, and gives us our sense of Us. Other parts reside internally, and guide us at other locations in our body. Some also sit on our skin.

Some of them have been with us in past incarnations, or iterations of our DNA.

When they get ignored or abused, the soul parts get 'sick' and give rise to dis-ease in the host, i.e., Us again.

Now, I am the first to agree that this might sound like a fancy of imagination, but by using a multi-soul-part model, I've ended up helping healing take place in the most unexpected ways. I have helped numerous people overcome procrastination and fears of moving forward as well as removing gluten intolerance and rashes on the skin. Remember, I do not market myself as a healer, I just help people I mentor get over obstacles that hold them back.

When we ignore relatively mild conditions, like a phobia, an intolerance, or allergy, we leave the door open for more insidious illnesses to visit our door. Non-debilitating dis-ease causes a disruption in our aura that sets up an imbalance in our triad of health.

The same is true of relatively innocuous thought patterns too, as mentioned in the chapter on wellbeing. Lack of love, excess of fear or worry, low self-esteem, and irrational anger are all seeds which can destabilise us so that we need to be healed.

If we just address the seed thought form, the healing is permanent.

MY DOWN TIME

On the whole, and touching a large piece of wood, I've had pretty good health all my life. I have only ever spent two nights in hospital, and that was one each on a shift pattern shared with my six other siblings, with each of my parents shortly before they passed away.

I've had to visit A&E twice to get patched up, but was in and out in a few hours. I've spent plenty of time visiting others in hospital and attending all sorts of appointments with healthcare professionals.

I rarely visit my doctor's surgery and actually see it as a place of last resort if I do get under the weather. My preference is to sort it out myself or go to one of several fabulous healers I know.

I do eat reasonably well, and walk the dogs daily, but have to admit to liking more units of alcohol a day than we're told we should imbibe. Warm English beer and cold New World wines are my tipples of choice.

My intuition is that, on balance, my system seems to operate well and that, when combined with a positive attitude, any transgressions against the advised norms are neutralised. All in all, I like to think, I do not represent a burden to the UK's hard-pressed National Health Service.

Furthermore, should I be unfortunate enough to succumb to any malaise, I would look to myself and my lifestyle first and take the drugs second.

I do, however, have a nagging problem with my right knee, which has been painful on and off since I was a child. It started when I got hit by a car. Something I hid from my parents and never went to hospital for. I remember that I had to hide a large bruise on my right hip for some time. The memory of why I felt I had to keep so quiet about it is a bit cloudy. It was something like not wanting to be told off for being so stupid.

Over the years, I had loads of tests for it and no cause could be found. During my forties, though, I found two amazing healers who helped me all but eliminate it. It can flare up big time, but just occasionally.

What made me realise that the pain in my knee had a psychological component, was one time when my Mum came to stay. She wanted some Reiki from me for a painful shoulder and asked if I could just use Roman Catholic spirits. When I told her that's not how it works, she said she wouldn't bother. Oddly enough, I didn't know how to comply with her request then, so was just being honest, but I reckon I could have a crack at that now.

Anyway, the next day, my knee felt really painful. When I mentioned this to the lady who was healing my knee at the next session, we discovered that not being believed was the trigger. Sure enough, since then if my knee flares up, I notice it's when I am being a bit contentious.

My knee was pretty fine until a few years later when I was approached by a TV company about creating a programme on practical applications of esoteric wisdom. At first, I thought they wanted me to be a programme consultant. After the initial meetings, it became clear that they had me in mind to host the show. My knee became more painful than ever. It was then that I also discovered that when I was being asked to step forward, that would cause pain in the leg with which I take my first pace.

Oddly enough, I am sharing stuff in this book that I have never shared before and it's holding up pretty well. There is light at the end of every tunnel.

BREADCRUMB: *if you have a pain or ache somewhere in your body, ask yourself a simple question. Is the pain in the affected area or somewhere in your head, which is perceiving the pain?*

THE CATCH

There is a fundamental limitation when it comes to healing. If the person who is being healed doesn't want to be healed, healing cannot be forced upon them. This principle applies to both conventional and alternative, or complementary, healing modalities.

Each of us can be equally effective at blocking the healing as we can at accepting it. Of course, there are people who do have illnesses and desperately want to be cured but can't seem to be. I don't profess to have any answers for these situations other than that there may be a karmic influence in operation.

Death is only a phase change and not final – people meet again and learn on each encounter. While this version of me and you might not return, our essence ripples down the timelines.

SELF HEALING

So, if you are afflicted by a pain, disease, or discomfort, the temptation is to take a pill or apply a cream to make it go away. I should point out that I am not a qualified medical professional and the information contained here is not a substitute for advice you should seek from a qualified doctor or physician. Just because I wouldn't take this course of action, doesn't mean you shouldn't, and this is just my personal view.

The way I deal with any dis-ease is to enter a dialogue with it, much as we can do with any of our thoughts. So I ask if it has a purpose. For example, there may be a pattern I am not seeing and a lesson to be learned. I cast my mind back to see if it has occurred before. If it has, I see if there is a trigger in my current life that has set it off. My knee pain is one example. I also get muscular pain in my abdomen sometimes when I am 'birthing' a book. A massage therapist specialising in working with pregnant women pointed this out to me.

If a trigger is spotted, then all we have to do is acknowledge we've spotted it, deal with the trigger, and the pain magically disappears. Note that this equally applies to spells of bad luck as it does to dis-ease.

If the pain stays, then I breathe into it and encourage it to leave. I thank it for coming along and give it my blessing to move on.

There is a way to transmute it on the way out too, but that's a bit too complex for this book, and something I teach practitioners.

Once the pain does leave, it's important to bring a replacement energy into the space it had occupied. There are a number of ways to do this. We can use healing energies from Reiki or even just the heat from a hot water bottle. Other mechanisms are the use of massage, light, sound, colour, and crystals.

Of course, if it doesn't clear up, go see someone.

| rebirth |

WHEN WE EMBRACE THE NOTION THAT ALMOST ANYTHING CAN BE HEALED IF WE DEAL WITH THE SEED CONDITION, AN EXCITING OPPORTUNITY FOR GROWTH AND EVOLUTION OPENS UP FOR US.

The vast majority of therapies and treatments are remedial. This means they wait for something to break, and then fix it. How would it be if we took ourselves as healed and whole just as we, are and then make ourselves even better?

Not only would this distance ourselves from the mind-set that we get old, ill, and die, it also opens us up to a new paradigm. As we get older, we can get better and better. While we may disintegrate eventually, we can delay the onset of the worst ravages of time and live in better health for longer. We can also help those who are younger with our wisdom and experience.

In the cycle of birth, death, and rebirth, what gives us the ability to have a new experience, so we can evolve at a soul level, is a new combination of DNA. We get a new name too, and born into a new part of the world with new people to interact with. Our memories are reset and we start all over. It's a system which isn't broken, it's how life works.

Imagine, though, if within a lifetime, we could upgrade ourselves at a fundamental level, without the inconvenience of death and rebirth. In the past, there hasn't been much time for this. Only two-hundred-or-so years ago, the average human life expectancy was between fifty to sixty years. It's reckoned that by 2050, women's average life expectancy will be around one-hundred. This gives us more time to experience life.

We will have more time to learn and more time to have multiple careers. Maintaining good health as long as possible becomes more of a priority.

When we learn to live magically, the world becomes kinder to us. Money, love, and opportunity all flow our way to take the pressure off. We enjoy better health and also begin to notice how a different kind of infection sets in. People around us start picking up on our vibe.

We become mindful of our existence and place in the world and how we fit in to the scheme of things with those around us. We also enjoy the fruits of timefulness.

We have space and time to do what we want and what we need to do and everything starts arriving just at the right time. This is not just opportunities turning up but also thoughts and enlightenments.

When we end up well-and-truly on path, life becomes a breeze and we can look away from remedial fixes and turn towards a generative future.

KINDFULNESS

One of the first opportunities living a charmed life gives to us is the ability to be kind to others. With spare capacity, we can give help to others. As we dispense acts of kindness, best done randomly, we find they ripple back at us faster than we can give them out. This is another example of a nice infection, as this effect spreads rapidly to those who benefit from our kindness. They find the world is kind to them too, and so pass this positive vibe onwards.

Once you have experienced this kinder world, there is no going back. It is self-serving as much as it serves others. By doing this, we are only being kind to ourselves.

Kindfulness doesn't mean you have to give all your worldly possessions and wealth away. Rather than giving out money, for example, a more valuable gift is sharing the knowledge of how to acquire it and keep it flowing. The same is true for love, time, and wellbeing. If you share that gift in exchange for a little money, it serves as a further example of how energy flow is important.

The ultimate form of kindfulness is one that we can bestow to ourselves that extends beyond our current incarnation. Each of us has the ability to heal the past and to influence the future. We have responsibilities that ripple across time.

RIPPLES IN TIME

If we imagine that where we are right now is a few feet above the centre of a lake, and we are holding a pebble … when we drop that pebble into the lake, it causes a splash and sends ripples out in all directions. If that pebble is a thought, the thought gets transmitted across the surface and eventually reaches the shore. In front of us is our future and behind us is our past.

Imagine then that we could do something right now that will help us immensely in the present, but also benefit our ancestors and descendants equally. This puts even greater onus on what we do and think right now.

What if the thought we held was this? We hold the responsibility in our hands right now for all the versions of us that have ever existed and that will ever exist. It is beholden on us to evolve to the highest state possible in this lifetime. As part of that responsibility, it is important not to take yourself too seriously, or feel that all the weight is on your shoulders.

It is incumbent on you to take this task on-board while you are also having fun and experiencing the best time of your life.

So, just imagine that your ancestors have been waiting patiently, locked in the past, for your realisation that you are about to release them from the chains that bound them. They did not have your wisdom, vision, and experience, although they contributed to them. Your descendants in the future are capable of evolving to a higher state too, but cannot begin their more advanced journey until you take your own chains off right now. These descendants, by the way, don't have to be blood relatives. They can be as influenced by the art you leave behind as the DNA trail you may seed.

This means, right now, the pebble you can drop is more like a rock!

DEATHLESS REINCARNATION

The first step in releasing this rock is to take off the layers and attributes you have adopted this far in your life. Think about all the character traits you exhibit that not only annoy others but that make you cringe too. If you can't think of them readily, just observe people around you, or characters on TV, that you don't like. Whatever it is that irritates you about them is a mirror you will find in yourself. If it doesn't bother you then it's not a trait you have to worry about.

UK readers especially, may know of both Ricky Gervais in The Office, and Steve Coogan's, Alan Partridge characters. Other readers, check them out on YouTube, as you will both laugh and cringe. I have wanted people to like me, gone over the top, just like them, and ended up embarrassing myself. Sometimes, I have found both characters hard to watch because I see a past version of myself in them so clearly.

Once we lose the layers we don't want or need any more, we can begin a process of rebirth. Wind the clock on until you are in a graveyard looking at your tombstone. You've just been a fly on the wall at your own funeral and listened to the eulogies. What's written on your tombstone, and what did they say about you?

What gap now exists between who and what you are now and what legacy and memory you would you like to leave behind?

It's important not to give yourself a hard time over this, or to feel a huge mountain has yet to be climbed, which is impossible in your remaining lifetime. Once that thought sets in, our best option is often to shed our current mortal coil and come back the conventional way down the birth canal to have another go.

Dream wild and dream big.

What qualities do you need right now so that this eulogy can be read?

What resources are required to land at your feet so that your promise can be delivered?

All we have to do then is send a message back in time to let our ancestors know we are on the case. Our future-selves will have already have picked this up and started pulling the strings.

Each day going forward, all we have to do is take one step, no matter how small, that helps us leave the most treasured legacy behind.

SOUL GROUPS

When we incarnate, one theory is that we agree what we will learn in our next lifetime and choose our parents to give us the DNA and upbringing required to give us the best shot. Another theory is that we attract the people around us during our lives that will help us with these learnings. These people must also want us in their lives to gain their life experiences.

As these types of theories are largely unprovable, there is no point putting energy into working out if they are true or not. If, however, they are a model that helps us understand why we are here and how we can make the most of our time here, they are useful allegories and metaphors.

It is thought that the people who are very close to us, and especially those who come in and out of our lives at random times, form our Soul Group. They may be unaware of each other and their individual roles, but they seem to be there just when we need them, or they need us.

Something rather strange happens when we make that decision to reincarnate within a lifetime. Some of our old Soul Group disappears, and we end up getting attached to a new group.

This is significant for two reasons.

First, we might think we've done something wrong when old contacts lose touch. In some cases, they might even take umbrage or think we have grown distant. This can be hurtful and cause us to doubt our course of action, which is also part of the learning.

The second reason is that the members of the new group have qualities, attributes, and connections that help you deliver your gifts in ways you could only dream of beforehand. When these new and helpful people show up out of the blue, it's a good signifier you are on path.

Such shifting between Soul Groups can also happen unconsciously. We might also reconnect with members of our old group once they go through similar upgrades at a soul level.

Just before you start deleting people from your phone book, remember that this is just a model.

A RUN IN WITH SPIRIT

I cannot readily remember when the events I am about to share started or when they largely abated. I am just sharing them in case they happen to you too, so that they don't scare you or make you worried. They are examples of spontaneous deathless reincarnation events that come along when we might least expect them.

It must have been a few years after I started meditating when I would be awoken some time between two and four a.m., and flashing and twinkling lights would appear all around me. They looked like snow flakes, and some people have told me they were angelic presences. I have no proof of this one way or the other.

Sometimes they would be extremely bright, and kaleidoscopic patterns appeared in front of and inside my third eye in the centre of my forehead. Sometimes the energies entered in the back of my skull. My body would be frozen to the bed and I felt I was being held down.

Some people might interpret what I experienced as interference from aliens putting probes inside my brain. At no time did I feel scared, although some mornings I would think, "Oh no, not again!"

Over the next few days, after a bout of these, I would find a client presenting themselves with a more complicated condition than I had ever seen.

From somewhere, a flash of inspiration would come along and I would 'know' exactly what to do to help them.

It seemed to me as if I had been reprogrammed and upgraded to a new level of 'software'. It might well have been angels or even my future selves, who knows? All I know is that I knew how to do something I had never been on a training course for, or read a book on.

Nowadays, I experience one of these 're-programmings' every odd month and I just know it will precede yet another new 'knowing'.

I've also experienced another strange 'other-worldly' form of possession. I share it with you again just in case it happens to you. I was about to deliver a new two-day workshop called Bending Time, and had gone out to walk the dogs by way of morning meditation. I mused on how best to kick the workshop off, when an aha moment hit me.

I realised in a flash that every one of my books explored an aspect of time, although I hadn't planned this when writing any of them, and had never connected them together. This gave me a nice story to tell for the workshop.

Just at the exact same time this idea arrived, I felt a presence about fifty-or-so metres behind me. I didn't turn around, but felt this 'thing' run full-tilt at me with enough energy that it penetrated my aura and fused with me.

I had heard of people having Near Death Experiences and coming back with new super-sensory skills. They talk of meeting spirits and angelic entities, and one of them 'walking back in' with them. They are called 'walk-ins'.

What I experienced was more like a 'Run In' and is an entity that is still with me now, smiling as I write this for being recognised for bringing in such a shift.

BREADCRUMB: *next time you receive a blinding revelation or realisation, welcome not just the idea on board but the messenger that brought it - be they real or ethereal. Show them your world, with all its current problems and opportunities, and ask them for advice and perspective.*

THE CATCH

Much of what I share in this chapter in particular is my own worldview, and my own experience. They just help me make sense of it all. When we incarnate on Earth, it's like someone dumped us here and threw away the Operator's Manual of how to run our lives. We have to work it all out again from scratch. It is no wonder we make mistakes.

One thing I do know, is that all our paths are different and there is no absolute right or wrong way to do things. When it comes to rebirthing ourselves without death, all we can do is hold the intention for transformation to occur. Whatever transformation comes along will be different for each of us.

If you don't experience flashing lights or 'walk-ins' or 'run-ins', you are not doing it wrong. Maybe you are just fine and it was me that needed the software patch installed.

So, the only catch with all of this is to try and predict or expect the mechanism by which the shift will occur.

GOALS OF LEARNING

Before I was introduced to goal setting, I must have been good at it already. Just about anything I could wish for or imagine had come my way. Of course, I could not wish to be doing what I am doing now, as I had no idea it could be done.

Someone introduced me to so-called SMART goals and I found I could manifest 50% of those goals too. I also learned why 50% of them didn't manifest. On the surface, SMART goals are quite good, and better than having no goals at all. There are several variations on this, but I was introduced to SMART as meaning Specific, Measurable, Achievable, Realistic, and Timed. These are all admirable and sensible attributes for any goal.

While there is nothing wrong with this on the surface, goals set in this manner are essentially limited by our imagination, experience, and the information to hand at the time they are set. Therein lies the flaw.

For example, you might write down a 'smart' goal as below, where the 'smart bits' are emboldened:

"By the end of June, I will have over **£10,000** monthly income, **net of tax**, from new clients buying my widgets at **£129.49** each. And each client will recommend at least **two other new clients** to me, so I can run my business by the end of the year from a **beach in the Bahamas**."

What's great about this is that it's a very specific goal. What's not so great is that, as a target-based goal, it restricts our options. There might be a better beach than the one we visited in the Bahamas on holiday (I have never been there). It may be that someone wants to buy a licence to manufacture your widgets for several million pounds, with an on-going royalty, so you afford to buy that beach and not work again.

The achievement of all you can possibly dream, and even more, is simpler than being as specific and focussed as this. All we have to do is to base our goal setting on what we would like to learn.

When you then align what you want to learn with what you want to achieve, something magical happens.

Firstly, you get presented with opportunities and challenges to help you grow as a person.

Secondly, the opportunities to help you achieve your goals appear as if by magic.

Thirdly, you achieve a level of results that are much better than you ever even imagined.

We get in the way of our own success, yet by stepping out of the loop and letting things arrive, we can reap untold benefits.

To set your learning-based goals, just write down three things you would like to learn in the next month, the next three months, the next year, and by the end of the next three years ahead.

Then write down what the most amazing result would be for you, for your family, for your business, and for the planet, when these goals and your learning come to pass.

By taking this less target-based approach, you are kinder on yourself by taking pressure off and you entangle yourself which a much more magical future.

In this new future, you will also learn that true peace and enlightenment comes from having no goals at all but, instead, allowing them to be set for you. Goals of learning, though, give us a nice transitional phase to pass through.

| the new magic |

THE TYPE OF MAGIC EXPLORED IN THIS BOOK IS NOT THAT NEW PER SE. AS I MENTIONED, ALL MAGIC CEASES TO BE MAGIC ONCE THE TRICK OF HOW IT IS DONE IS KNOWN AND UNDERSTOOD.

What is new, is the context in the way the magic can be used and what it can be used for. With greater understanding, perspective, and sagacity, we can utilise this form of magic in new and innovative ways.

Many thousands of years ago, such magic was only used by those blessed with a propensity for the dark and white arts at birth. Everyone else feared and revered it.

When the great religions arose, they locked the magic away in vast libraries lest it undermine dogma. Practitioners were forced 'underground' and invoked their magic in private, as so many of their peers were tortured and killed. When science became the New Religion, magic was derided as bunkum and driven further underground.

Over the last thousand years, humans have achieved mastery over the Physical Plane. By looking inside the atoms we are made from, and outside at the universe we live in, we understand much about how we came to be here. This mastery has come at a price. We have separated from Source.

A Theory of Everything still proves elusive and science readily admits it still has those 'hard questions' to answer. Much of the universe appears to be missing, and we are a long way from understanding how we came to be conscious and self-aware. We have, however, discovered – or re-discovered – a phenomenon called entanglement, where two particles separated from each other 'remember' each other. If you ascribe to the Big Bang theory, at one point, everything was connected to everything else. It still is, as we are.

The answers to some of science's last remaining conundrums can be found in esoteric writings. The mystics and sages 'knew' some of the answers, but had neither the language to explain it clearly, or the mathematics to model it. They could only use glyphs and codings as their metaphors. This was also how they hid the secrets from those who were not ready.

So the 'new magic' is all about integration and openness. Throughout the ages, magic has been used with good and nefarious intentions. Those who have used magic to better themselves at the expense of others, will have had to learn a lesson in one life or another.

The real lesson is not a wrap on the knuckles or the breaking of a wand, but the understanding that magic comes through us, not from us. Once we are entrusted with one level of magic, more and more skills and different abilities are conferred upon us.

For magic and science to merge, the traffic has to go both ways. I look forward equally to the New Scientist magazine turning up each week on my iPad Newsstand, as I do my monthly gems of wisdom arriving from The Builders of the Adytum. The latter still arrive by post.

Scientists can find tomorrow's physics in yesterday's metaphysics. Conversely, those practicing and dabbling in the esoteric arts can learn much from the latest scientific research. In the same way, Eastern and Western medicine can be forged together so that 1+1=3. Science needs magic as much as magic can really benefit from the Scientific Method.

THE META-SCIENTIFIC METHOD

We can be forgiven for thinking that the Scientific Method is something that was developed relatively recently – say, since the Industrial Revolution. In fact, it has been in common use for thousands of years. It's often said that Aristotle was its progenitor, but who actually introduced it has been lost in antiquity. It's more likely that it fell into common usage because any other methods led to less successful results.

It is essentially common sense. If you think about it, it's how we are programmed to learn from the moment we leave the womb. Here's how it works in essence:

Step 1: You observe or notice a new phenomenon, or a pattern, and you try and make sense of it.

Step 2: You form an explanation, theory, or hypothesis. This can take the form of an analogy or metaphor like 'riding a beam of light' or a mathematical equation like $E=mc2$.

Step 3: You make a prediction based on your theory.

Step 4: You measure and test against your prediction.

Step 5: If it's successful, you shout "Eureka" and, if not, you go back to Step 1 or 2.

When it comes to developing 'magical' techniques, this is a pretty good method to follow. It leads to consistency and improvement via trial and error. It then becomes something that is teachable and shareable.

This method can be extended with a sprinkling of magic.

We can use our ability to connect with our future self to generate the aha moment as a precursor to Step 1. This Step Zero can also come in the form of a seed in a dream.

We can use that same ability to 'channel' the future in a further Step 6. Our same ability to experience aha moments on demand can be used to be innovative around the applications for, and spin-offs from, our discovery.

When we entrust we are on the right path, these revelations will appear at our doorstep, especially if we are holding the highest good for our inventions and innovations.

MAGICAL APPLICATIONS

The bridging of magic and science can extend further than just with the generation of ideas.

While the geneticist might seek to modify an organism by tinkering with a gene, an esotericist would use mindful meditation to effect the transmutation. This might be implemented by a thought form, and perhaps amplified by a 'spell'. Other alchemical helpers such as symbols, crystals, and sound can also be used.

While the mechanisms may not be understood, I have seen miraculous healing take place in front of my eyes. I've seen skin rashes disappear, gluten intolerance leaving, and even the healing of burns awaiting skin grafts. While some of these are not necessarily genetic in nature, they demonstrate that we can 'magically' manipulate organic matter.

As we are organic in nature, we have a natural influence over other organic matter. I am sure this involves communication at a chemical, biological, and auric level.

With a little more attunement and practice, we can influence inorganic matter too. The efficacy of drugs could easily be enhanced if they were imbued with healing energy. Indeed, the drug itself might even become a placebo.

Applications also exist outside the sphere of healing.

Both our brains and micro-electronics work at a quantum level. Some marvellous conventional science is being done right now to control machines with brain waves. From learning mind control via an interface, our brains evolve and it is a small step to lose the interface entirely.

In finance, governments use quantitative easing to print more money when the wheels fall off the bus. This mechanism would not be needed if money was seen as an energy, and not an object. Rather than devaluing money, it can be used as a force with which to deliver our promise, both individually and collectively. How and what we spend money on, affects how it allows its energy to amplify rather than dilute. This will need both fiscal policy change at one end and education of individuals at the other.

My current field of research into our relationship with time has huge implications for both productivity and our longevity. Time is only as fixed as we make it, and we all possess our own Time Machine: our minds. When we change our mind, we change our time. It's not so much that we get more done in less time, but that we generate more time in which to get things done.

MY KIND OF MAGIC

My introduction to this magical world came from some training sessions I attended with magical people. Incidentally, I noticed that the trainers I learned the most from were sorceresses, rather than sorcerers. I know this is significant in two ways.

Firstly, that female magicians are intrinsically more powerful than males. Secondly, my particular set of skills resonate more with the feminine that the masculine energies. You could even go as far as to postulate that my breed of magic is typical of what happens when a male works with feminine energies.

I should emphasise that I attended both these training sessions primarily from the perspective of research. The last thing I was expecting, or even seeking, was for my inner magician to awaken. Through a combination of attunements, initiations, practices, and study, after just a couple of years, I became a different person.

What I learned from this is that these super-sensible skills are dormant and nascent in all of us. We are of course free to ignore them, or fear them, and hence suppress them. When we accept them as our birth-right however, and find the right teacher, they come to the surface naturally. The other realisation about magic is how nicely infectious it is. Hang around with magical people, and magic pops into your world.

Through these initial awakenings, I found out there are thousands of talented and magical people all over the world. Many of them work in isolation, with their clients coming via word of mouth. Some open schools and provide training courses. Some, bizarrely, think their magic is the only magic and start to trademark healing modalities and methodologies. When old-school fear-based thinking mixes with new thought, it rarely ends well.

It didn't take me long to realise that what I wanted to learn could not be found in one particular place. I found study of the Tarot useful, yet I intuitively felt the Western Mystery tradition was somewhat linear. Other schools of wisdom felt somewhat ungrounded, as lovely as they are.

At first, when things don't exactly fit, we feel that something is wrong with us and we're not doing things quite right. It dawned on me that everyone has a different path and there is no one-size-fits-all. This is, of course, why religions come a bit unstuck. We have all taken a myriad of paths to get to where we are now and have a myriad of paths yet to take.

After some years of introspection and retrospection, it became clear to me that my particular skill set and experience allowed me to act as a bridge. I had a fabulous grounding in the physical sciences and was adept at using the Internet. I'd also learned much about the publishing process.

I could use this mind-set to embrace esoteric wisdom and translate it into something both comprehensible and practically useful.

My prowess in all things 'Interwebby', combined with this new experience in publishing, was the icing on the cake.

Before I knew it, a portfolio of books appeared, along with eLearning courses, to expand and demonstrate what I was writing about. I also transformed fully from a broadcast engineer to a broadcaster, or at least a narrowcaster. I started a podcast show where the whole topic of conversation was to bring magic into the open.

My new mission appeared in front of me rather than me having to find it. I was to take the esoteric and make it exoteric.

I know that this represents only small beginnings.

BREADCRUMB: just imagine what type of magician you would like to be. Think of a particular 'super power' that you would like to invoke, then imagine how you could use it to help others. Then just let it arrive, in this life or the next.

THE CATCH

When we begin to live a magical life and bring magic into our world, common sense can zoom out of the window. I know of some people who buy wands and wizard's hats and cloaks. The true magician breezes in and out of our world without us realising it until they have gone.

It is of vital importance that we should never become self-important. We are only entrusted with as much magic as we can handle. To become more magical, we must demonstrate we can use our current skills wisely and not to better ourselves at the expense of others.

There is also another insidious side effect from opening up our magical powers, which I observed when both attending and delivering workshops. Most attendees extend what they are capable of in some form or other and learn new ways to interact with the world. While their ability to manifest positive change increases, the potential to invite less desirable events to occur also increases.

I always advise people who attend my workshops of this potential, and to thank adversity should it appear. Firstly, it represents an opportunity for growth. Secondly, it proves what a good manifestor they have become. I also remind attendees that there is no such thing as negative energy or a negative thought form. It is just positive energy pointed in the wrong direction, or a positive thought form which has not been well formed.

BE YOUR OWN MAGICIAN

The very last thing I want from anyone reading this book is to copy or follow me. This is one of the very reasons I've not written about this subject to date. Each of our paths is different and that's all part of the plan. By exploring our own route through life, collectively we learn so much more.

In the same way that we are better at some subjects at school or one sport or another, we have natural strengths in different types of magic. Like heptathletes ... some, of course, will be all-rounders.

A great way to discover what your natural flair is, is to try a few things out. By taking a healing session, you can see a practitioner in action and also naturally will pick up on their 'vibe'. There are innumerable half-day workshops, where you can pick up a new skill. Increasingly, you will find resources online too.

Some people will be naturally clairvoyant and be able to 'see' through the veil of illusion. Some have a heightened sense of touch, being clairsentient. If you hear voices, you are clairaudient. Others that are claircogniscent will just 'know' stuff that they know they didn't know. There are those too, who can taste and smell, being clairgustatory and clairolfactory.

Most people will have some mix of these sensitivities.

For example, I am primarily claircogniscent with a sprinkling of clairvoyance and the odd bit of clairaudience. If I wanted to become more clairsentient, I know of ways to enhance these skills. This is like a 400 metre runner knowing they could also run 10,000 metres, but also knowing it is not for them right now.

Whatever propensity you want to develop, it's important to have fun and not to put yourself under pressure. Whatever you do, do not compare yourself with others. Whatever talents we have are just the ones we are meant to have at any one time.

| the new era |

YOU WOULD BE RIGHT TO ASK WHAT IS THIS NEW ERA THE BOOK TITLE ALLUDES TO. WELL, SINCE THE DAWN OF MANKIND, PROBABLY EVERY GENERATION HAS CLAIMED THAT SOMETHING MOMENTOUS IS ABOUT TO HAPPEN TO THEM.

In days of yore, messages were seen in the stars with comets and planetary alignments. These days there are no end of people proclaiming that the world is about to end or that a new phase of humanity is about to unfold.

The 21st of December 2012 came and went without a whimper. The man-made date of the year 2000 hardly ruffled a feather or caused a computer glitch. I know of one large corporate running an old version of Windows, who got around it by winding all the computer clocks back to 1990. The point being that, when dealing with such portents, it is wise to use some objectivity and sanity. When it comes to foretelling what is going to happen to us and our planet, two major factors should be born in mind.

The first is that humankind represents the merest fraction of the biomass of the planet. If we wiped ourselves out tomorrow, life on earth would continue just fine without us. Mass extinctions have happened before on the Earth and will undoubtedly happen again.

The second factor to consider is that life as we know it is not limited to incarnate three-dimensional forms, such as plants, insects, animals, and us. We are all three-dimensional distillations and projections of multi-dimensional intelligences. We live in a very pervasive illusion we call reality. With just a little training and attunement, we can peer through the veil.

It is fair to say though that we do have a special place in that reality, as we seem to be the only beings on this special planet with enough 'smarts' to reverse engineer the possible meaning of Life, The Universe, and Everything.

Indeed, our mastery over the Physical Plane allows us to see out into the void and potentially spot incoming objects that might wipe out life on the planet. We may even develop the capability to deflect stray meteorites and Earth-bound asteroids.

At the same time, we have tools and intellect to look within. We have mathematical models that support the theory that our three dimensions of space and one of time are indeed the tip of a multi-dimensional iceberg.

This new era is one which brings a new level of realisation. When we appreciate that the cosmos is alive and that all stars, planets, and moons have a level of consciousness, the veil of illusion can part. Our possible role in the order and place of things can emerge.

What if we are a special aspect of the whole gamut of things whose task is to look back at the Universe and work all of this out? What if we are children of the cosmos who incarnate with the mission to explore what is possible when higher dimensional intelligence descends into the Physical Plane?

We can then enter this new era and take on a new level of responsibility. Rather than just being passengers on Spaceship Earth, we can take on a role as caretakers and guardians of this special place we call home. We can, will, and should look out into the outer cosmos, and even send probes out as our emissaries.

At the same time, we must explore inner space too. This is the inner space between atomic particles that represents 0.000001% of matter. It is from within this space that what appears to be the new magic appears.

In the next century, we will begin to comprehend how consciousness is not an epiphenomenon, or offshoot, of the world around us. Awareness is intrinsic to the fabric of space-time. It is also thought in some metaphysical circles that awareness came first and crystallised and distilled itself into the material world, as incarnate beings.

This process is ongoing and higher level consciousness still can become incarnate as our 'vibration' increases. As it does so, our capabilities are augmented. We can even get involved with the process.

To begin to imagine what this all means, just take an imaginative journey back a hundred years. We go back to a world that we can easily envisage as we've seen it in newsreels and on films. In the so-called Western World at least, we had the motorcar, powered flight, electricity, telecommunications, healthcare, widely available education, and sanitisation. We also were extending the other measure of technology considerably. We could kill each other at increasing distance away from each other.

In the First World War, no longer did we have to see our opponent to kill them with an arrow or a bullet, we could map where they were and send a shell over 30 kilometres to land on their heads. These days, a remote operator can fly a drone and land a bomb with pinpoint accuracy on the other side of the planet.

Just imagine if that same technology could be used to send supplies such as food and medicines. It is such a shift in thinking that is now within our grasp.

The world we enjoy today is a spin-off of technologies imagined by our ancestors. We can now speak to anyone anywhere on the planet with a connection to a mobile phone network. We can see inside our bodies without the use of a scalpel.

With a smartphone and an Internet connection, we can broadcast a message to billions of people.

Just like the minds of a century ago, which dreamt of a rocket going to the Moon, we can dream up possible futures for both ourselves and the generations to come.

What if that future was one that we create utilising our untapped potential? What if we fully realised that if we can imagine anything, it can happen? All we have to do is to allow it to arrive, while being careful and mindful of what we wish for.

OUT WITH THE OLD

I saw a fabulous play a few years back called *All New People*. The overarching message was that in one-hundred to one-hundred-and-twenty years or so, everyone on the planet will be new. This means they can have a new crack at everything and they don't need to continue with old ways that don't serve them any more.

When complex societies first formed, the method of government was usually an autocracy. In some less-than-forward thinking countries, it still is. The head of such an autocracy is often given their role by birth-right; sometimes by bloody means. The autocrat, backed by advisors and an often-ruthless militia, makes up and maintains the rules. When a populace is largely uneducated, this system at least gives some sort of framework for everyone to operate within.

Autocracies morphed into plutocracies, where the power was held by the wealthy. This would be a mixture of landowners, and the church would be in the mix somewhere as the spiritual advisor. Until republics came about, often through revolution, the top landowner within the plutocracy often became the autocrat.

Only in the last few hundred years, has democracy become commonplace. Here, the leaders are, in theory, ordinary people voted into power by other ordinary people.

No system of government is without its flaws and anomalies. The UK is perhaps as weird and convoluted as they come. Although I live in a modern democratic country, it is headed up by the Queen who is an autocrat. The government rules with its strings often pulled by wealthy plutocrats. At least I am free to write this paragraph without living in fear of incarceration, or worse.

The coming century will see the rise of the meritocracy. In this model, the people with the talent to run affairs rise to the top. Ideally, this process should be democratically controlled. Some of those acting as leaders will have skills in running government, budgeting at a national level, and with foreign policy. Some will be technically and even militarily adept. Undoubtedly, religious leaders will continue to provide moral and spiritual direction and governance.

Initially, democracies will morph into meritocracies at a national level. Some of the Scandinavian countries have already made such transitions. Increasingly though, we are seeing movements of people who are thinking globally. The most notable are trans-national organisations like Greenpeace and Amnesty International. These fine institutions battle with the old regimes.

The most exciting initiatives lay where the old rules can be rewritten from the ground up. A great example of this is the crowd-funding movement where many individuals fund innovative and fun ideas that banks see as too risky. By spreading risk so no individual funder can lose much money, the risk actually disappears.

You can register your computer to become part of a global cloud, processing large amounts of data. Your spare computer capacity might find extra-terrestrial life, spot an Earth-bound asteroid, or discover a cure for cancer or dementia.

The wisdom of the crowd offers so much potential, mostly yet untapped. A greener, kinder, more empathetic world is opening up for the next group of All New People.

IT MATTERS TO THAT ONE

There is a well known tale worth retelling here. A man comes across a small boy on the beach. The beach is littered with starfish that have been washed up by a strong tide. The boy is tossing starfish back into the sea.

The man says, "What are you doing?"

The boy answers, "Saving the starfish."

The man says, "You are wasting your time, you can never save them all."

The boy tosses another back, and replies, "I might not be able to save them all, but I can save this one."

The man then joined the boy in throwing them back into the sea.

One of the comforting aspects of living in a democracy is that we can leave the tough decisions to people we have voted in. As I live in an area where the current MP has a vast majority, there is little point in me even voting. Until proportional representation comes in, these anomalies will continue to exist.

In a meritocracy, we all have a voice and can all make a ripple. We don't have to wait until political systems change either.

As we are all wired together through the collective consciousness, we can effect change merely by all pulling in a similar direction, with a cohesive mind-set.

It's said that when a hundred monkeys on one island pick up a new skill, like getting insects out of a tree by dipping a stick in honey, monkeys on neighbouring islands separated by water, pick up the same skill.

So imagine enough people just get bored with war and stop playing violent computer games. Imagine if we replace obsession with over-eating with a desire to feed the world. Imagine if we take more responsibility for our own wellbeing. Such individual initiatives have the potential to scale up globally.

The pervasiveness of the Internet and social media helps us spread the word and share best practice. While this might sound naive and a bit of a pipe dream, every disruptive change and memorable event in history started with a dream.

If we all dream in the same direction, the shift will happen.

BREADCRUMB: *if you were to reincarnate on the Earth plane in a future life, what sort of world would you like to come back to? What could you do right now to help that sort of world come to be?*

SPACESHIP EARTH

One thing every person on the Earth shares with each other is the planet we live on. It, of course, makes a lot of sense to look after it, as it's the only place we know about that we can feasibly live. The very concept of a national boundary makes little sense in this context. I don't readily know how we can transition to global citizens other than I don't think of myself as British but as a human sharing a ride on a Special Spaceship.

This Spaceship has its own life support system and a bio-system that keeps us alive. We can no more think ourselves separate from each other than we can be separated from the biosphere. Take out the nematode worms that munch through the detritus from the surface and we'd all be dead within a few years.

This book has primarily dealt with how we can all elevate our consciousness with new super-sensibility. What happens when enough 'monkeys' on this Spaceship Island wake up is that the first domino in a line falls over and takes the rest with it.

Each species and group of species, like us, also possesses a collective consciousness too. When we upgrade, all species groups get an upgrade too.

Our Mother Earth also has a level of awareness. When we go up a gear, she too jumps up a level or three.

Likewise, each planet in our solar system and each star system, has an awareness and intelligence sometimes referred to as a 'logos'. They are all connected together. When the Earth upgrades, she will send ripples around the cosmos.

As self-aware individuals then, we have a responsibility on our shoulders. When we shift, everything shifts.

Wanna play?

| thanks |

THIS BOOK CAME ABOUT BECAUSE OF THIS
SEQUENCE OF EVENTS.

Julia Lee flipped some sort of vibratory switch in me
during an amazing Reiki session.

Lisa Turner introduced me to the concept of
meditation and suggested that I read A Key to the Wisdom
of Ages by Paul Foster Case.

I vibrated some more when I read this book and it
connected me to the Builders of the Adytum in California.

Through Lisa, I met the humangel Wendy Salter and
reconnected with the lovely Denise Harris-Heigho. They
both initiated me to a new level of being.

Through meditation, I accidentally channelled my first
book, 100 Years of Ermintrude.

That first book connected me with the very special Jackie Walker. Everyone needs a Jackie to blether with on their journey in order to keep them sane and on path.

Jackie Walker connected me with Lea Woodward, who spotted something big and significant that I had overlooked.

Although by the time I spoke with Lea, I had written 10 books, I had not told my story or shared any of the real secrets that I had discovered.

It was that conversation that lead directly to this book being written. Everyone needs a Lea, too, to help them see the woods from the trees.

There are some others I must thank too, for helping me get to write this book. Some of whom have left the Earth Plane, and others who are still active in it.

Thanks to Harmony Kent for her attention to detail.

Thanks to Sabine Sangitar and Pia So'Sua from the Kryon School in Germany.

Thanks to Lita de Alberdi for strengthening and deepening my channelling skills.

Thanks to Lilou Mace for entitling an interview with me with a strapline that inspired this book.

Thanks to Sue Warwick, Sherry Wakeman, and Tina Fotherby for helping me step out from the shadows.

Thanks to Paul Foster Case, Rudolph Steiner, Emmanuel Swedenborg, Thomas Aquinas, Ganesh, and Hermes for sharing your wisdom when you were down here.

Thanks even more so for your gentle guidance and constant nudging from where you are now.

| tomography |

TOM EVANS IS AN AUTHOR, HOST OF THE ZONE SHOW PODCAST, AND THE CREATOR OF LIVING TIMEFULLY, THE WORLD'S FIRST MINDFUL APPROACH TO TIME MANAGEMENT.

His passion is taking the esoteric, or unknown and hidden, and making it exoteric, or known and understood. As an ex-BBC engineer, he was fascinated by the magic of television. Nowadays, he is intrigued by the magic of the mind and the hidden potential we can all tap into.

His books explore what it means to be human and how we can become super-sensible.

He lives in the Surrey Hills with his life partner and dogs. His four legged companions take him for a walk when they sense he is in need of a shot of inspiration.

| bibliography |

NON-FICTION WORKS AVAILABLE IN PRINT AND FOR
EREADERS

Where is The Zone?
How do we get in it?
What do we do when we are out of it?

*"A few of the Zones hit a raw nerve.
It reminded me to be kinder to myself.
Recommended for anyone who would
like to live a charmed magical life."*

The Zone

Ever wondered where ideas came
from and how to stop the best ones
from getting away?

*"... a fabulously evocative book full of humour,
wisdom and insight. Simply inspiring ..."*

The Art & Science of Light Bulb Moments

We are only limited by what
we imagine.
So just turn everything up
a gear or three.

*"This We Are takes the concepts seeded in
This We know to new heights & into new realms
of possibility ... and probability"*

This We Are

An exploration of what we know,
what we don't know and what sort
of world we could know ...

*"... short, elegant and perfectly formed.
A small book with a big impact ..."*

This We Know

An immersive guide to clearing
writer's block and unleashing
your Creative Muse ...

*"... packed with practical techniques to
ensure your blocks are a thing of the past"*

Blocks

A contemporary exploration and exposition of the wisdom contained in the Major Arcana of the Tarot ...

"... this has become my go-to book any time I need guidance and support"

Flavours of Thought

Hidden in the Minor Arcana of the Tarot is the secret of who we really are and where we might be going ...

"... another mind-bending and inspiring read. Get ready for a wild ride."

Planes of Being

SHORT STORIES FOR EREADERS

A poetic trilogy about one family
told in just 99 stanzas ...

"Stunning. I cried. That's all."

100 Years of Ermintrude

A future history of planet Earth,
how we got here and where we
might be heading ...

*"A good page turner and syfy at it's best,
a book I'll re-read again and again."*

Soulwave

Twenty two short, beguiling stories to
open your mind and change your world

*"This book gives us the encouragement to
step up and step out so we can live our lives
out loud in ways we may not have thought
of before ..."*

The Germinatrix and other tall tales

AWAKEN YOUR
INNER MAGICIAN

Lightning Source UK Ltd.
Milton Keynes UK
UKOW06f1849010515

250760UK00008B/58/P